Conditioning *for*
FIGURE SKATING

OFF-ICE TECHNIQUES FOR ON-ICE PERFORMANCE

CARL M. POE, M.S., C.S.C.S.

Contemporary Books

Chicago New York San Francisco Lisbon London Madrid Mexico City
Milan New Delhi San Juan Seoul Singapore Sydney Toronto

Library of Congress Cataloging-in-Publication Data

Poe, Carl M.
    Conditioning for figure skating : off-ice techniques for on-ice performance / Carl M. Poe.
        p.   cm.
    Includes index.
    ISBN 1-57028-220-X (alk. paper)
    1. Skating—Training.   2. Physical fitness.   I. Title.

    GV850.4 .P64   2002
    796.91′2—dc21   2002022257

Contemporary Books

A Division of The **McGraw·Hill** Companies

1 2 3 4 5 6 7 8 9 0   QPD/QPD   1 0 9 8 7 6 5 4 3 2

ISBN 1-57028-220-X

Interior photographs by Matthew Georgopulos
Cover photograph copyright © Anton Want/Allsport

McGraw-Hill books are available at special quantity discounts to use as premiums and sales promotions, or for use in corporate training programs. For more information, please write to the Director of Special Sales, Professional Publishing, McGraw-Hill, Two Penn Plaza, New York, NY 10121-2298. Or contact your local bookstore.

The purpose of this book is to educate. It is sold with the understanding that the publisher and author shall have neither liability nor responsibility for any injury caused or alleged to be caused directly or indirectly by the information contained in this book. While every effort has been made to ensure its accuracy, the book's contents should not be construed as medical advice. Each person's health needs are unique. To obtain recommendations appropriate to your particular situation, please consult a qualified health care provider.

This book is printed on acid-free paper.

Contents

Preface

The popularity of the sport of figure skating has grown tremendously over the past five to six years. With skating shows in almost every major city and increased television coverage, more young kids are being exposed to and becoming interested in skating.

Learn-to-skate programs at skating rinks throughout the United States are a breeding ground for young skating talent. To be competitive, children begin their on-ice skill training as early as five years of age and spend many hours every day on-ice. The sport demands both a tremendous amount of physical work (for technical merit) and artistic style. *Conditioning for Figure Skating* deals with the physical preparation of the preliminary through senior and elite skater involved in all disciplines of figure skating—singles, pairs, and ice dance. Competitive skating has changed dramatically with a greater emphasis on technical aspects, such as triple and quadruple jumps and triple-triple jump combinations for singles, dynamic lifts and jumps for pairs, and dynamic free-dance maneuvers in ice dancing. Tremendous physical capacity is needed to skate a long program and complete that last triple jump or double combination and end up with a good-quality spin. A skater's heart rate can reach over 190 beats per minute. Strength, power, flexibility, balance, aerobic endurance, anaerobic endurance, and muscular endurance all play a huge role in the success of a well-skated program.

Off-ice strength and conditioning training should be mandatory. Being an off-ice strength and conditioning coach for many years, I have seen an increased need for off-ice training. I have watched a scrawny thirteen-year-old novice men's skater go from barely performing a clean double axel to executing a huge double axel and three different triples in less than a year and a half. In two seasons this skater went from not even qualifying for the U.S. National Championships to winning the novice men's national championship title the following season, thus qualifying for junior world tryouts. Off-ice, his strength and power increased tremendously to values unheard of for a fourteen-year-old male skater. Specifically, his dynamic vertical jump went from 15.5 inches to 21.5 inches in two years, and his hard work off-ice resulted in injury-free training on-ice for that time period.

It is unfortunate that some skaters still do not perform off-ice strength and conditioning training. Occasionally, a skater will get by without any supplemental training. But to rely on skill work alone on the ice is not enough to fully enhance or prolong the injury-free career of a skater, no matter what his or her level.

Coaches, parents, and skaters need to realize that a stronger skater can acquire skills on-ice at a faster rate and reduce the risk of skating-related injuries. Assuming that on-ice techniques have been taught properly, the stronger, better-conditioned skater should be able to stroke faster, spin with better control, jump higher on the ice, rotate faster, and land with greater strength and stability. Coaches, parents, and skaters can use this book to supplement the physical preparation of the skater, including proper warm-up drills, flexibility stretches, cool-down routines, strength training, jump and plyometric training program design, and endurance conditioning program design for on-ice injury prevention and enhancement of skating performances. The guidelines and principles give a clear understanding of the program design. Techniques are described and illustrated so that any coach and skater will be able to implement the program and benefit from this training structure.

Not only does *Conditioning for Figure Skating* provide the various components for off-ice and on-ice supplemental training, it provides you with a yearly plan to maximize your training potential through periodization. Chapter 8, which covers periodization, is unique in that it details the phases of off-ice training to provide for a peak in physical performance for the competitive figure-skating season for the juvenile through senior-level and elite skater.

Acknowledgments

During my years as an off-ice strength and conditioning coach, many individuals have given me the opportunity to continue my education in figure skating and coach skaters throughout the United States. Through the years, it has been challenging to develop, implement, and manage off-ice strength and conditioning training for all levels and disciplines of figure skating. There are a few coaches, officials, committee members, and skaters that I would like to thank:

- Christy Krall, national program director, United States Figure Skating Association (USFSA), who has taken it upon herself to implement various sports science camps and related programs for skaters throughout the United States. I have been involved in many elite camps and national camps as well as other related programs that Christy has organized. Her dedication to the sport has resulted in tremendous gains in the sport sciences and in strength and conditioning training opportunities for U.S. figure skaters.

- World and Olympic coach Don Laws, who was one of the first coaches to get me involved in figure skating and with sport science and strength and conditioning training of skaters; also, world and Olympic Coach Kathy Casey, who gave me the opportunity to train and develop elite figure skaters at the World Arena, Broadmoor Figure Skating Club, and Colorado Springs World Arena; and Tom Zakrajsek, national- and international-level coach, who has been very receptive to off-ice strength and conditioning training for figure skating.

- ∞ Mike Stone, Ph.D., and Harold O'Bryant, Ph.D., both professors at Appalachian State University, and J. T. Kearney, Ph.D., United States Olympic Committee, who have given me the education to develop my resources.

- ∞ USFSA Sports Medicine Committee members Dr. Howard Silby, Dr. Ed Reisman, Dr. Mahlon Bradley, Dr. David B. Coppel, and Debbie King, Ph.D., who have all been extremely resourceful with sports science and sports medicine information related to skating throughout the years.

- ∞ Mrs. Carolyn Kruse, who has served on many committees at USFSA headquarters and has always been supportive of my work in helping skaters with off-ice training.

- ∞ I would like to acknowledge master-rated coach Robyn Petroskey-Poe of Buffalo Grove, Illinois, for technical material pertaining to on-ice stroking patterns and drills for endurance conditioning for the figure skater.

- ∞ To the individuals that perform and put the end product on the ice: Mr. Daniel Lee, who always gave 101 percent effort throughout the three years that I worked with him—his hard work in the weight room resulted in significant gains on-ice; Miss Sydne Vogel, who always brought a positive attitude to her off-ice strength and conditioning training; Mr. Evan Lysacek and Mr. Ryan Bradley, who both brought excellent exercise technique, hard work, and a great sense of humor to the weight room; and to Matthew Georgopulos, whose photographs throughout greatly enhanced and amplified the text.

- ∞ And finally, to Matt Savoie and Sarah Hughes and the many levels of skaters— preliminary, senior elite, Olympic, world, and international—who I have worked with throughout the years. Their commitment and desire to better themselves physically and emotionally for their sport has definitely been appreciated. Even though there have been some hurdles and challenges to physically prepare these skaters, there is no substitute for the joy of seeing skaters of all levels benefit from off-ice strength and conditioning—be it enhancing lifting technique, increasing resistance on a certain exercise, or landing a jump on the floor—and then seeing the finished product on the ice, with skaters successfully completing skills that they struggled with before becoming stronger and better conditioned. Thanks to all you skaters for your effort.

- ∞ I would like to further acknowledge Debbie King, Ph.D., biomechanist, Montana State University, Bozeman, Montana, who has contributed a lot of her research to the USFSA, and who contributed to Chapter 1.

Introduction

$\mathcal{T}$he sport of figure skating has taken on an incredible new look with the skating performances of today's athletes. Actually, it is just now that figure skaters are being recognized as athletes and figure skating as a sport. The abilities of some of today's elite skaters are unbelievable. The triple jump is no longer the benchmark since quad rotational jumps have come into the picture. Demanding four-minute programs with seven to eight triple jumps, some being triple-triple combination jumps, are now commonplace. However, we must step back and look at how young talented skaters are introduced to the sport, develop throughout their skating years, and maintain their skills once they are at their peak. Unlike many other sports, figure skating yields highly talented technical athletes as early as ten to sixteen years of age. These young skaters must be able to continue their skill work and competitive skating performances for many years.

What can this do to the body? How can grassroots skaters enhance their chances of developing these sport skills (stroking, spinning, jumping)? How can prepubescent girls keep developing their skill work, especially jumps, as they begin to develop into adolescent skaters? As a strength and conditioning coach involved in the sport of figure skating for the last nine years, I have examined many practices, studied many videotapes of jumps and other program work, and worked many competitions. I have talked to many coaches, officials, judges, and skaters regarding various aspects of the sport. Overall, I have seen major changes and approaches within the sport. As it relates to enhancement for sports performance, the main problem that I have noticed with figure skating is a simple lack of education.

SKATING PERFORMANCE OF AN ELITE INTERNATIONAL-LEVEL SKATER

So many coaches and skaters have used on-ice skill work alone for their overall athletic skill development. Practicing skill work on-ice alone *will not* better condition the skater; it will not increase strength, power, flexibility, muscular endurance, aerobic endurance, and anaerobic endurance. All these components come into play when a skater competes. For the senior elite skater to successfully perform five to six triples, combination jumps, and dynamic spins with speed and do this with artistic appeal, his or her physical capacity must be trained.

How many times have you seen a skater in practice land all his jumps, spin with good control and speed, and stroke fast? This skater may also complete each skill with great ease, power, and strength. However, when this skater puts the pieces together into one four-minute program with added technical choreography, he struggles. He starts off his program strong, but due to a lack of muscular strength, power, and especially conditioning, he fades. This skater misses those last few elements, falls on jumps, rushes his spin, is slow in stroking, and finishes gasping for air. This can be true for both elite and novice skaters. Lack of strength, power, and endurance conditioning can be relative to the level of the skater. These lacks are especially apparent in juvenile- and intermediate-level skaters who do not have the strength and power to complete a lot of the required jumps (such as single axels or double jumps) or jump combinations.

The present state of figure-skating training requires more than attending daily practice sessions and just jumping, spinning, or running through your program. The purpose of this book is not to develop world and Olympic champions, but to provide the necessary tools that juvenile- to senior-level skaters can use to enhance their physical performance and

U.S. ELITE-LEVEL SKATER STRENGTH TRAINING
An elite, international-level skater performs a back squat strengthening exercise. The off-ice strength coach is spotting this athlete for safety and to ensure that he is utilizing correct exercise technique.

prevent skating-related injuries. If they do find themselves taking the ice for world or Olympic competition, hopefully they will do so injury free and in better physical condition than their competitors.

I feel strongly that off-ice strength coaches must target and set obtainable objectives for preliminary-, juvenile-, and intermediate-level skaters. The simple philosophy of my program is that if the skaters that I train can increase their physical work capacity through off-ice training, then their skill acquisition may increase at a faster rate. Finally, if these skaters are stronger and better conditioned, the risk of skating-related injuries is less, and if there is an injury, recovery is faster. My most important objective is to prolong the injury-free skating careers of all levels of skaters. Hopefully, coaches, skaters, parents, officials, and even judges using this book will understand better the importance of off-ice strength and conditioning training. This book can provide a conditioning plan for the coach and skater. The supplemental drills given in this book will enhance the development of a skater's on-ice skating skills and elements. The programs are designed to be specific and simple, with emphasis placed on proper technique, safety, and overall progression. And remember, it is well documented that the stronger, more conditioned skater has greater self-esteem, and is more confident in her or his performance.

Conditioning
for
FIGURE
SKATING

CHAPTER 1

Physical Components of Figure Skating

To be successful in any sport, an individual must be able to perform repeatedly at his or her highest skill level and ignore any physical distractions, such as fatigue, stress, and minor injury, during a competition or throughout the training season or year. Sport-specific skills can be lost if a person is not in peak condition. What does it take physically to perform a free-skating program, free-dance program, or a pairs long program? What components of training should be used to enhance the preparation for these performances? Before answering those questions, skaters and on-ice technical and off-ice strength coaches must do a needs analysis of the skater within his or her specific discipline: singles, pairs, or ice dance. The needs analysis determines the following for the skater:

- Biomechanical movements used in performing skills

- Physiological components used to produce these skills and to produce them within a program

- Common sites of injury relative to the sport

BIOMECHANICAL ANALYSIS

To assess what specific areas of strength and conditioning training a skater should utilize, the coach must determine which movements to train; for example, the biomechanical movement patterns of a triple axel for singles, a triple twist for pairs, or edge quality and

1

SKATER PERFORMING A TRIPLE JUMP ON-ICE
Notice the physical strength and power this skater exemplifies during this jump.

stroking movements for ice dancers. Biomechanics involves the muscle and joint patterns needed to perform a certain skill. It is important to analyze the movement patterns on-ice before designing and implementing a strength program. Not only do you have to distinguish among differences in disciplines, but also among differences in levels of skating within each discipline (for example, the skill level of a juvenile skater compared to a novice skater). Tables 1.1 to 1.3 describe the body and joint areas used in the three disciplines of figure skating and the joint and muscle areas that should be strengthened.

LAYOVER CAMEL SPIN
Balance and flexibility are both important dynamics of the layover camel spin position.

TABLE 1.1	SINGLES BODY, JOINT, AND MUSCLE AREAS	
Body Area	*Joint Area*	*Muscle Area*
Upper	Head	Neck, trapezius
Upper	Shoulder	Deltoids
Upper	—	Lattisimus dorsi, pectoralis major
Middle	Hip	Abdominal, lower back, torso
Lower	Hip	Gluteals
Lower	Knee	Quadriceps, hamstrings
Lower	Ankle	Gastrocnemius, soleus, or calves; tibialis anterior/ posterior, peroneus

PAIRS LIFT
Strength and power are shown in a pairs lift.

ICE DANCE
This ice dance maneuver displays the dynamics of this discipline of figure skating.

TABLE 1.2   PAIRS BODY, JOINT, AND MUSCLE AREAS

Body Area	Joint Area	Muscle Area
Upper	Head	Neck, trapezius
Upper	Shoulder	Deltoids
Upper	Elbow	Arms: biceps and triceps
Upper	Wrist	Wrist, forearm
Upper	—	Lattisimus dorsi, pectoralis major
Middle	Hip	Abdominals, lower back, torso
Lower	Hip	Gluteals
Lower	Knee	Quadriceps, hamstrings
Lower	Ankle	Gastrocnemius, soleus, or calves, tibialis anterior/ posterior, peroneus

TABLE 1.3   ICE DANCE BODY, JOINT, AND MUSCLE AREAS

Body Area	Joint Area	Muscle Area
Upper	Head	Neck, trapezius
Upper	Shoulder	Deltoids
Upper	Elbow	Arms: biceps and triceps
Upper	Wrist	Wrist, forearm
Upper	—	Lattisimus dorsi, pectoralis major
Middle	Hip	Abdominals, lower back, torso
Lower	Hip	Gluteals
Lower	Knee	Quadriceps, hamstrings
Lower	Ankle	Gastrocnemius, soleus, or calves; tibialis anterior/ posterior, peroneus

The complexity of analyzing figure-skating movements on-ice can be better understood by analyzing a videotape of a skater's work or program run-throughs. Each skating discipline can obviously yield different movement patterns when an element is performed. For example, through research we know that multirotational jumps (singles and pairs application) depend a lot on the muscular action of the shoulder, hip, and knee joints.[1]

For on-ice rotational jumps, strong neck and upper back muscles are needed for head stabilization while a skater is rotating. Shoulders and the upper back (latissimus dorsi) contract to pull the arms in for rotation and keep them in while rotating. Also, strong upper back and shoulders are critical for arm extension in landing position or checking out. Chest strength is needed for muscular balance to the upper back musculature. Abdominals, lower back, and/or the torso area are used for torso positioning before the skater leaves the ice for a jump, for trunk stabilization while in rotation, and for stabilization while in landing position. This area is also known as the core of the body. This is an extremely important area for the figure skater to strengthen because a lot of skating skill movements depend on the stability and power of this area.

Lower body musculature—the gluteals, quadriceps, and gastrocnemius and soleus areas—is needed for the explosive push off the ice on jump takeoff. Muscles of the hip and upper legs are used for leg stabilization and for creating the adducted or crossed-leg position while in rotation. Finally, the hamstrings play a key role in eccentric stability as a skater lands a jump and for all deceleration of jump takeoff and landing.

In summary, one can see how biomechanics relate to the strength needs of a skater. How to build these strengths will be detailed in Chapter 3.

The following outline lists the muscles involved for various figure-skating skills, as well as areas for strength training and possible flexibility training.

1. STROKING

A. PROPULSIVE MUSCLES
1. Hip extension and abduction (gluteals, muscles of pelvic area, hamstrings)
2. Knee extension (quadriceps)
3. Ankle extension; plantar flexion (gastrocnemius, soleus)

B. STABILIZING MUSCLES
1. Trunk
   a. Abdominal (rectus abdominus, obliques)
   b. Back (erector spinae)
2. Gliding or skating leg
   a. Hip gluteals, quadriceps, muscles of the pelvic area
   b. Knee (quadriceps)
   c. Ankle (gastrocnemius, soleus, tibialis)
   d. Balance; fine control (anterior tibialis, posterior tibialis, gastrocnemius, soleus, peroneus)

    e. Ankle inversion (posterior tibialis)

    f. Ankle eversion (peroneus longus)

    g. Arch support, ankle structure (gastrocnemius, soleus, plantar fascia)

2. JUMPING

A. PROPULSIVE MUSCLES (TAKEOFF)

1. Hip extension (gluteals, hamstring)
2. Knee extension (quadriceps)
3. Ankle extension; plantar flexion (gastrocnemius, soleus)

B. OTHER CONTRIBUTING MUSCLES

1. Hip flexion for free leg, edge jumps (illiopsoas, rectus femoris)
2. Shoulder flexion and adduction (pectoralis, anterior deltoid, and coracobrachialis)

C. STABILIZING MUSCLES

1. Abdominal (rectus abdominus, obliques)
2. Back (erector spinae)

D. ROTATING MUSCLES (SPINNING)

1. Shoulder adduction (coracobrachialis, pectoralis, anterior deltoid)
2. Shoulder transverse adduction (anterior deltoid, pectoralis major)
3. Elbow flexion (biceps, brachialis)
4. Hip adduction (adductors)

E. LANDING MUSCLES

1. Hip flexion; extensors eccentrically (gluteals, quadriceps)
2. Knee flexion; extensors eccentrically (hamstrings)
3. Ankle dorsiflexion; plantar flexors eccentrically (contract to absorb or accommodate force of landing, where the body is trying to decelerate)

F. TRUNK STABILIZATION

1. Abdominal (see above)
2. Back (see above)

3. LIFTS

A. LOWER BODY

1. Hip extension (gluteals, hamstrings)
2. Knee extension (quadriceps)
3. Ankle extension

B. UPPER BODY

1. Shoulder flexion (anterior deltoid, coracobrachialis, pectoralis)
2. Elbow extension (triceps)

C. STABILIZATION
1. Trunk
   a. Abdominal (see above)
   b. Back (see above)
2. Shoulder girdle (rotator cuff)
3. Wrist

Another factor, which is very important, is the energy needed to perform the necessary skill movements and elements on-ice.

Energy is the ability or capacity to perform work. The type of physical activity—its duration and intensity—determines which energy system is used: aerobic or anaerobic.

Aerobic. The aerobic system kicks in when the body uses oxygen for three minutes or longer; it supplies long-duration energy. This system primarily uses carbohydrates and fats as substrates for energy production.

Anaerobic. The anaerobic system functions without oxygen. It produces a high amount of energy and fatigue waste products, such as lactic acid (anaerobic glycolysis), which accumulate in the muscles and blood. The anaerobic energy system can supply immediate energy for a duration of zero to ten seconds or intermediate energy lasting up to two to three minutes.

Anaerobic ATP-PC (immediate energy: zero to ten seconds). These immediate energy sources are chemical reactions in the muscle (cell) where adenosine triphosphate (ATP) provides energy quickly for muscular contraction.

Anaerobic glycolysis (intermediate energy: from ten seconds up to two to three minutes of high-intensity movement). This system relies on carbohydrates as a substrate for energy production. Carbohydrates are broken down and stored in the muscles and blood, thus readily available for energy production for muscle contraction.

PHYSIOLOGY OF SKATING

How much energy does a skater need to complete a two-minute short program or a long program lasting over four minutes? Currently, researchers are trying to determine which system figure skating uses more—aerobic or anaerobic—when it comes to energy production.

Obviously, the technical components of a skater's program will dictate its relative intensity and thus which energy system is predominately being utilized. As a skater performs his or her program, three energy systems (anaerobic ATP-PC, anaerobic glycolysis, and aerobic) are active. Table 1.4 presents a breakdown of various program components and their respective energy sources for a junior elite skater competing at the 2001 Junior World Championship.

Referring to Table 1.4, you can see that any skater or coach can determine the specific time/durations of a skater's program. With a stopwatch and videotape, calculations of the skills performed within the program can be determined. This can be very helpful in developing specific strength, power, and conditioning training for that skater's program

TABLE 1.4   SKATING SKILL WORK AND ENERGY SYSTEMS OF A
PROGRAM LASTING THREE MINUTES, THIRTY-SIX SECONDS

Skill Performed	*Energy Source Component*	*Skill Durations*
6 triple jumps, 2 double jumps	Anaerobic (immediate): 0–10 seconds	5.09 seconds (average of .63 second for each jump executed)
Continuous stroking, skating, crossovers, choreography	Aerobic and anaerobic glycolysis: 2–3 minutes	121 seconds
Footwork: one short sequence	Anaerobic (immediate): 0–10 seconds	22.28 seconds (average of 11.4 seconds)
3 spins: flying camel, layback, combination spin	Anaerobic (immediate): 0–10 seconds	26.25 seconds (average of 8.75 seconds per spin)
Spirals and/or spiral sequence: includes spread eagles, bauers, arabesques	Aerobic: duration can vary	19 seconds
Dynamic elements: includes hops, half-loop jump tuck-up, stars	Anaerobic (immediate): 0–10 seconds	8.57 seconds

Total Time: 3.36 minutes

because you know which energy system and which components (strength, power, flexibility) to train and how long to train each skill duration.

The more dynamic the program, the higher the relative intensity, thus the more time the skater spends in producing energy via anaerobic sources. This holds true for all three disciplines of skating: singles, pairs, and ice dance. All components—speed of skating, number and difficulty of jumps, pair lifts, throw jumps, dance lifts, movements, footwork, dynamic spins—will affect the energy demands of the program. Another component affecting program intensity is the technical aspect of the choreography. A skater using demanding choreography with a lot of dynamic arm, hip, head, and torso movements will utilize more energy than the skater with less technical choreography.

As mentioned before, researchers are currently determining the relative intensities (aerobic and anaerobic) of skating short and long programs. However, previous research has indicated that skating requires maximal to supramaximal physical capabilities, resulting in a rapid accumulation of fatigue waste products (lactic acid) in the muscles, possibly reducing the ability of the skater to complete elements of his or her program.[2] Through practical on-ice program testing, I have measured many skating programs via use of a heart rate monitor. The pattern that exists and is consistent with the research is that a skater's heart rate reaches maximum levels quickly (within one minute) and stays elevated for the whole program. Thus, skaters are expected to complete all planned jumps and elements with style/choreography while undergoing high physiological stress. How to address this need and train the appropriate energy systems will be discussed in Chapter 6.

COMMON INJURIES

Throughout the years, I have seen an unbelievable number of skating-related injuries. Research shows that the following are the most common skating-related injuries:

- Chronic overuse injuries, such as tendonitis of the lower leg and knee area and lower back pain
- Stress fractures, especially of the ankle, foot, and lower leg
- Acute injuries or fractures and sprains, especially in the lower back, hips, knees, and ankles[3, 4]

Overall, skating-related injuries stem from damage to the muscle, bone and/or soft tissue (tendon, cartilage, or ligaments). I have noticed that many practice hours spent on-ice repeatedly performing the same maneuver cause most chronic overuse injuries. Acute injuries result from practicing rotational jumps while fatigued or attempting jumps or other elements that are too difficult for a particular skater. Ill-fitting boots and overtraining, especially for prepubescent skaters (eight to twelve years of age), can lead to injuries. Finally,

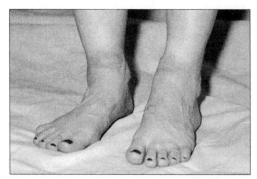

Years of boot-related stress to the foot/ankle area are evident in the feet of this ex-elite figure skater. This skater went through twenty-five pairs of boots during her competitive career.

the highest incidence of injuries occur in the months of September and October (which is the preseason or regional qualifying training period). During this period, some skaters increase total jump volume and frequency of program run-throughs, but fail to schedule enough recovery or rest days to physically and mentally regenerate.

HOW DO SKATERS PROTECT THEMSELVES FROM RISK OF INJURY?

What can skaters do to prevent these injuries or at least lessen the severity of an injury? The best way to prevent injury is through physical preparation, equipment preparation, and relative technical on-ice progression.

1. Proper warm-up and cool-down before and after training and competitions
2. Strength training
3. Flexibility training
4. Proper equipment (boots, blades)

5. Proper progression with on-ice skill technique
6. Periodization of training, both on-ice and off-ice (especially adding rest and recovery periods and balance of training from on-ice skill work to off-ice training)

Physical preparation entails an adequate warm-up and cool-down routine that includes flexibility stretching. Also, skaters must utilize strength training throughout the duration of their competitive careers. There is no doubt that the stronger a skater is at each joint (neck, shoulder, lower back/hip, knee, and ankle), the less likely he or she is to incur an injury that keeps him or her off the ice missing training time. Also, if the skater incurs an injury, higher strength levels (including muscle, bone, and soft tissue, tendon, and/or ligament strength) may enable that skater to recover quicker and return to on-ice training.

Selecting the proper boot plays an important part in injury prevention for the figure skater. Boot size and texture (stiff or soft) should be appropriate and specific to the skater's individual needs. Doing lots of lower leg and foot strengthening and flexibility exercises is one important way to prevent lower leg and ankle injury from the boot. Once the boot is laced up, there is very little ankle flexion/extension, inversion/eversion, or overall movement. Because of this, the lower leg and ankle can become weaker despite all the hours spent on the ice. Therefore, during off-ice training, the skater must continually work on flexion, inversion, and eversion strengthening exercises and especially dynamic exercises such as low-intensity plyometrics for the lower leg.

The volume of training has a direct impact on injuries. Research has indicated that skaters spend an enormous amount of time on-ice, practicing skill work and running through programs.[5] Top-level skaters may dedicate up to six and a half hours per day on the ice, five to six days a week. This can add up to nearly 1,500 hours over a competitive season. Obviously, competitive skaters train year-round; however, the actual competitive season may last one to four months, depending on the success of qualifying. These days, juvenile, intermediate, and novice skaters are spending from eleven and a half to twelve hours weekly on-ice. This much training, especially jump repetition, can be detrimental to skaters, especially prepubescent skaters who are still growing and developing. The coach, skater, and parent must ask what is the appropriate amount of training volume needed relative to overall training time to maximize skill acquisition, yet reduce the potential for staleness, plateauing, overtraining, and, of course, injury.

As a strength and conditioning coach and educator for the skating community, I find it ironic that some coaches and parents feel that off-ice strength training, such as lifting weights, can be dangerous for young skaters. However, young skaters may be on the ice for three freestyles a day— "pounding" jump after jump (double flip, double lutz, maybe double axel), attempting jumps that are too difficult and spending more time falling on the ice than landing, and doing excessive program run-throughs. So what is appropriate for on-ice training volume and skill progression? Lately, periodization training (see Chapter 8) is becoming more popular in sports training throughout the United States, Europe, and other countries. This method structures a skater's supplemental training to peak physically and prevent overtraining. Periodization for on-ice training involves manipulating or varying the following:

1. Volume or duration of total on-ice training time
2. Intensity or degree at which skaters attempt various jumps and pair lifts
3. Volume of the total attempts on jumps
4. Volume of the amount of program run-throughs
5. Frequency of field moves, choreography, and ballet, and supplementing with other skating-related components
6. Rest

Coaches need to design on-ice training that stresses the athlete with skill work, yet varies the program with other supplemental drills and allows for recovery from the more intense technical work (jumps); for example, supplementing a high-volume jump session on-ice with field move drills.

Keep in mind that modification of the above mentioned variables could take place daily, weekly, and monthly. Periodization is also good leading up to specific competitions and after major competitions. To summarize, the ultimate goal for the coach is to prepare his or her skater to be in peak condition on-ice and fully rested before major competitions. Not only should that skater be at an appropriate peak in skill level, rested, and on-ice injury free, the physical peak in performance should be instilled. Chapter 8 describes in detail off-ice and on-ice physical preparation (peaking).

In looking at the whole picture, the physical components needed for any skater—preliminary to senior elite—to enhance on-ice training and competition performance while resisting injury include the following, as listed previously:

1. Proper warm-up and cool-down before and after training and competitions
2. Strength training
3. Flexibility training
4. Proper equipment (boots, blades)
5. Proper progression with on-ice skill technique
6. Periodization of training, both on-ice and off-ice (especially adding rest and recovery periods and balance of training from on-ice skill work to off-ice training)

These training components must be used consistently and be specific to the skater. The warm-up and cool-down routine, strength training program, jump/plyometric program, endurance conditioning, and all included component techniques need to be specific to the biomechanical and physiological parameters of the program, whether singles, pairs, or ice dance. Since skating relies heavily on artistic and aesthetic impression, physical preparation of the skater must be specific to those needs. A strength coach should not overtrain a skater and create a hypertrophied, overly muscled individual, unless it is deemed necessary (such as for a male pairs skater). Program design must be individualized, meeting the specific needs of a skater. Obviously, ice dancers will not prepare the same way as singles and pair skaters.

What is our final goal? No matter what the discipline, the skater must be in top skill and physical condition while remaining injury free for performance.

CHAPTER 2

Warm-Up, Cool-Down, and Flexibility Preparation

Every time I am at an ice arena, I am amazed at how many skaters arrive at the rink, get out of the car, walk in, put their skates on, and take to the ice without any warm-up and stretch routine. I even see this at competitions! If there is ever a need for an appropriate off-ice warm-up and cool-down it is at competition time. A competition event is stressful. Implementing the appropriate warm-up and cool-down routines throughout the week can clearly give skaters an edge over their competitors.

THE WARM-UP: THE SKATER GETS READY

On-ice skaters have only six minutes to warm up and prepare for their jumps, spins, lifts, and dance movements. Skaters can have an advantage if they properly warm up off-ice prior to their on-ice warm-up. Also, coaches and skaters must use warming-up, stretching drills, and specific drills in certain situations, such as when a skater may be the last or next to last to skate. Certain strategies may make the difference in that skater's physical readiness.

What is a proper warm-up routine? How do skaters benefit from warming up? A figure skater's warm-up can be divided into two parts.

General Warm-Up. The general warm-up consists of five to eight minutes of aerobic activity, such as jumping rope, using a slideboard, jogging in place, or box/bench step-ups, followed by at least ten to twelve minutes of total-body flexibility stretches of each joint area—neck, shoulder, elbow, wrist, hip/torso, low back, knee, and ankle.

Specific Warm-Up. The specific warm-up uses movement patterns that closely simulate the sport. Unfortunately, a majority of skaters do not perform this warm-up.

The specific warm-up can be divided further by the three disciplines: singles, pairs, and ice dance. The following is a list of some examples of specific warm-up movements for each discipline.

Singles. Dryland air turns, rotational jumps, low-intensity plyometric jumps/movement, choreography program run-throughs.

Pairs. Dryland air turns, rotational jumps, pair lifts, low-intensity plyometric jumps/movements, choreography program run-throughs.

Ice Dance. Low-intensity plyometric movements, dance lifts, choreography program run-throughs.

Keep in mind that a skater's off-ice warm-ups will vary. If a skater has a difficult on-ice program, then a longer off-ice general and specific warm-up is needed. Skaters with long programs definitely need to spend more time warming up off-ice than those with short programs.

Physiologically speaking, both the general and the specific warm-ups provide a number of benefits. Overall, skaters who do an aerobic activity, stretching, and dynamic movements during an off-ice warm-up will receive the following benefits:

1. Increased heart rate and blood flow
2. Increased core muscle temperature
3. Increased speed and strength of muscular contraction and relaxation (needed in jumps, spins, footwork, and stroking)
4. Enhanced exchange of oxygen to the working muscles
5. Increased activity in both the brain and the lungs, thus enabling more efficient use of oxygen and improved breathing, which enhances endurance capacity
6. Increased coordination
7. Reduced risk of an on-ice injury

Taken together, these benefits will enable the skater to perform his or her on-ice skill work more efficiently and quickly.

Flexibility Training

Not only is flexibility stretching an important part of a skater's warm-up routine, it is also a necessary component of off-ice training. Some skaters may get plenty of flexibility training from ballet classes; therefore, their off-ice training can target more strength, power, and endurance conditioning. However, flexibility stretching should be required after any type of exercise stress or on-ice skating. All skaters should be doing total-body stretching five to six days per week. Postpractice and off-ice training sessions are an excellent time for flexibility training because the skater's body or muscle and joint temperature is at a good state for increasing range of motion.

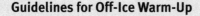

Guidelines for Off-Ice Warm-Up

During both prepractice and precompetition off-ice warm-ups, the skater should do the following:

1. Perform the warm-up in a comfortable environment, such as a warm-up room or locker room, or out by the ice or rink area.

2. Perform the warm-up on a soft landing surface (wooden floor, ballet floor, mats, rubber, or matted flooring) with adequate space.

3. Wear appropriate footwear (cross-trainers or high-top or midcut basketball shoes) with good heel/ankle support.

4. Include one aerobic or body movement activity to increase heart rate and body temperature, causing a mild sweat but not fatigue.

5. Include static (slow, controlled joint/muscle stretching or range of motion) flexibility stretching of the total body; stretches should be held for at least ten to fifteen seconds and may be repeated.

6. Perform specific movements that closely simulate on-ice performance.

7. End the warm-up at least ten to fifteen minutes before taking to the ice for practice or competition warm-up; this leaves enough time to lace up skates and mentally prepare.

8. Keep warm after the warm-up by wearing proper clothing and not sitting down or standing still; continue to move the upper body (arms) and middle and lower body (legs).

Surprisingly, the problem with some skaters is not inflexibility but too much flexibility at certain joint areas. A skater that is too flexible, or laxed, may have a greater risk for injury than the skater that is inflexible. There needs to be a balance between stretching and strength training to maintain or promote joint stability. Keep in mind that correct strength training technique will also increase joint and muscle range of motion or flexibility. How do you avoid becoming too flexible? Some skaters are born with great flexibility; what they are lacking is sufficient strength training for the joint areas. Skaters that are too laxed or flexible should stretch minimally and increase their frequency of strength training off-ice to increase joint and muscle integrity along with strengthening the soft tissue (ligaments, tendons, and cartilage).

Overall, if skaters use flexibility stretching as part of their off-ice warm up, stretch after practice sessions and after all off-ice training, and are involved in ballet training, their flexibility needs will more than likely be met. The skater could stretch roughly two to three times per day and hold stretches for ten to fifteen seconds before practice and competitive programs and one minute after those programs. Coaches and skaters must realize the importance of targeting areas of possible muscular imbalance, previous injured areas, or areas of joint and muscle tightness. Flexibility training for the skater ensures the following:

- Decreases susceptibility to injury

- Increases efficiency of movement to execute skills more effectively

- Facilitates coordinated movements, which aids other athletic parameters, such as strength, power, speed, and agility

- Enhances the skater's body lines and choreographed movements

GENERAL AND SPECIFIC WARM-UP ACTIVITIES AND FLEXIBILITY STRETCHES

The following section illustrates off-ice warm-up exercise techniques. Both general and specific warm-ups may vary depending on the level of the skater and the duration and technicality of the skater's competitive program. Thus, not all skaters would perform the following drill sequences. Finally, variables such as a competitive schedule, injury status of the skater, and overall energy level of the skater must be taken into account.

General Warm-Up Activities (*Duration five to eight minutes*)
Choose one activity or a combination of the listed activities.

JUMP ROPE
Note the skater's body alignment and landing on the balls of the feet.

BENCH STEP-UPS
Total-body warm-up drill that can be done on steps at the rink or on benches.

CARIOCAS OR CROSSOVERS
Note the control of the skater, staying on the balls of the feet. This is a total-body warm-up drill with emphasis on the hips, legs, torso, and arms.

JOGGING IN PLACE
This activity can be done at any ice rink. The skater can jog in place or jog around the rink lobby or around the rink area.

Flexibility Stretches *(Duration approximately ten to twelve minutes)*
Try to perform all stretches or a combination of the stretches.

NECK CIRCLES
Slow, controlled rotation of the head to stretch the muscles of the neck; perform clockwise and counterclockwise.

ARM CIRCLES
With arms fully extended, rotate in large circles with a slow and controlled movement; perform clockwise and counterclockwise.

SINGLE-ARM PULL
With the free arm, pull the opposite arm, which should be fully extended, across the midline of the chest. This is an excellent shoulder and chest stretch.

OVERHEAD TRICEPS PULL
Note the skater reaching behind and pulling the arm at the elbow joint downward slowly. This skater is stretching the arms, shoulders, and upper back muscle groups.

ARMS IN TO CHEST
Dynamic calisthenic movement for the arms, shoulders, upper back, and chest. The skater should perform approximately five movements.

TRUNK ROTATION
Rotation movement of the trunk. Another controlled movement for the torso, hips, and lower back areas.

CROSSED-LEG HAMSTRING STRETCH
With legs crossed, this skater is slowly reaching with extended arms toward her feet. Excellent stretch for the hamstrings and lower back. Make sure to switch legs to stretch the opposite leg.

SINGLE-LEG QUAD PULL
Balanced stretch of the hip and quadriceps or upper leg.

CALF PUSH
The skater is stretching the lower leg or gastrocnemius and soleus muscle groups. Notice the skater pushing against the wall, with shoulders square, good back alignment, and the rear foot flat on the floor with the leg straight.

ACHILLES TOE STRETCH
With the toe high on the wall, the skater is stretching the lower leg and ankle area, especially the Achilles tendon complex.

Left.

Right.

STRADDLE SIT-N-REACH
These three stretches involve the straddle position on the floor. Notice that the skater sits on the floor with legs extended, toes pointing toward the ceiling. The skater reaches for each foot. These positions are excellent for the hips, hamstrings, groin area, and lower back.

Center.

PIKE REACH
The skater, with legs straight and a flat back, reaches for the feet to stretch the hamstrings, lower back, and hip area.

SUPINE KNEE FLEX
Lying in a supine position, the skater pulls the leg toward the chest or midline of the body to stretch the hip flexors. This can also be a good partner stretch.

SUPINE HAMSTRING PULL
In the same position, the skater pulls the straight leg back, making sure the back is flat on the floor, with the opposite leg slightly bent at the knee. This is a great stretch for the hamstrings, hips, and lower back.

BUTTERFLY
With legs tucked in and a flat back position, this position stretches the groin area. To increase the range of motion, the skater can press down on his or her knees and push the thigh toward the floor. This will increase the stretch at the groin or inner thigh area.

FOOT CIRCLES
This movement involves pointing the toe and rotating the foot in a large circle. The skater should have a good sitting posture, relaxing the ankle and rotating the foot approximately five times both clockwise and counterclockwise.

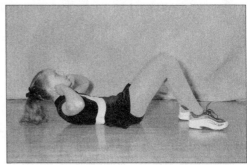

ABDOMINAL CRUNCHES
The skater is using crunches, another dynamic movement, to provide a stretch at the abdominal area. Note the position of the skater: hands are behind the ears with elbows out, and knees are bent with feet flat on the floor. The movement lifts the shoulder blades off the floor and then back down. Skaters should perform approximately ten repetitions.

BACK EXTENSION
This is also called the seal stretch. With legs and hips flat on the floor, extend the arms as if pressing out of a push-up position. This is an excellent total-body stretch of the hips, lower back, arms, shoulders, upper back, and chest.

SPIRAL STRETCH
This is a skating-specific stretch movement. Note the position of the skater to simulate a spiral balance position on the floor. Make sure the skater performs this on the opposite leg for cross-balance stretch. Overall, this is another total-body stretch involving legs, hips, lower back, arms, shoulders and upper back.

Specific Warm-Up Activities *(Duration at least fifteen to eighteen minutes)*
Tables 2.1 and 2.2 list warm-up activities specific for singles, pairs, and ice dance. Following each table are photographs illustrating those activities. Volume (sets and repetitions) and rest periods of the specific warm-up may vary. Repetitions equal the number of foot contacts or number of times the skater touches the ground.

Warm-Up Activities for Singles and Pairs
Along with the activities listed in Table 2.1, pair skaters would also use this time for specific off-ice warm-up of their pairs lifts. Both singles and pairs skaters would end their off-ice specific warm-up with dryland choreography program run-throughs.

TABLE 2.1   SINGLES AND PAIRS

Activity	Sets	Repetitions	Rest Period
Ankle bounces	2	6	1 minute
Double-leg lateral jumps	2	6	1 minute
Single-leg skip bounds	2	6	1.5 minute
Crossed-leg torso rotations	2	10	30 seconds
Simulated axel/double axel takeoffs	2	5	—
Floor landing position	2	5	—
Jump, air position landing	2	5	—
Quarter air turns (double-leg landing)	1	1	30 seconds
Quarter air turns (single-leg landing)	1	1	30 seconds
Single loop jump	1	2	30 seconds
Single axel jump	1	2	30 seconds
Doubles (loop, flip, lutz, double axel, or triple rotations)	1	2	30 seconds
Dryland program run-through	—	—	—
Dryland pairs lifts	—	—	—

Start position. **Finish position.**

ANKLE BOUNCES

This is a dynamic low-intensity plyometric exercise for the ankle, lower leg, and arms. Note the skater extending the ankle and the nice vertical (extended) position in the air. Emphasis should be placed on a quick takeoff from the floor, takeoff and landing on the balls of the feet, and finally with a jump with maximal height, using a quick double-arm swing.

Start position. **Finish position.**

DOUBLE-LEG LATERAL JUMPS

The skater is performing a low-intensity plyometric jump; the emphasis is on extending the ankle, knee, and hip. The skater should bend the knees, drop the hips, and jump to the side, landing the jump and quickly accelerating into another jump takeoff in the opposite direction. Make sure the shoulders and hips are square and that the skater involves the arms on takeoff.

Start position. **Finish position.**

(handwritten: Z 6 / S r)

SINGLE-LEG SKIP BOUNDS
This is a power movement where the skater jumps off the single leg by extending the ankle, knee, and hip, using a double-arm swing, jumping off the floor with one leg, landing on the same leg, and quickly accelerating into another takeoff from the opposite leg. This drill is for maximal vertical height. Note the complete body extension of the skater.

CROSSED-LEG TORSO ROTATIONS
The skater is isolating the torso area by stabilizing the hips and rotating the torso in a twisting motion. Note the "in-air" rotation position of the legs and arms. The key is to minimize action of the hips and just concentrate on movement of the torso or middle body.

(handwritten: Z 10 / S r)

Start position.   **Finish position.**

SIMULATED AXEL/DOUBLE AXEL TAKEOFFS
The skater simulates an axel takeoff on the floor trying to extend off the takeoff leg, making sure she uses an explosive movement of the legs and arms. This drill is for maximal vertical height and not rotation.

Start position.   **Finish position.**

FLOOR LANDING POSITION
The skater is performing a check-out (landing position) on the floor from a closed rotation position while on the floor. Emphasis should be placed on quickness of the free leg and arms extending out to a nice landing position and an appropriate knee bend in the landing leg.

Start position.	Middle position.	Finish position.

JUMP, AIR POSITION LANDING

The skater is performing a maximal vertical jump while simulating an in-air position with a single-leg landing. Make sure there is a closed air position (legs tight in the air) before the single-leg check-out on the floor.

Start.	Quarter turn.	Half turn.	Three-quarter turn.

QUARTER AIR TURNS (DOUBLE-LEG LANDING)

These are sequential jump air turns in which the skater lands on both feet. The skater begins the air turn in the direction (clockwise or counterclockwise) she rotates on-ice: she performs a quarter turn, then jumps back the opposite way. The skater next performs a half turn, and a three-quarter turn, each time jumping back in the opposite direction. Finally, she makes a full single turn or rotation, again jumping back in the opposite direction. Make sure the arms pull in and extend on landing and landings take place on the balls of the feet.

Start.   **Quarter turn.**   **Half turn.**   **Three-quarter turn.**

QUARTER AIR TURNS (SINGLE-LEG LANDING)
The skater is performing air turns with a single-leg landing. Concentrate on a quick free-leg and arm extension, while allowing for a good knee bend of the landing leg.

Start position.   **Finish position.**

SINGLE LOOP JUMP
The start position of the single loop jump is shown, followed by the landing position. Try to make the jump big, using power from the legs and arms.

Start position.

Middle position, back view.

Middle position, front view.

Finish position.

DOUBLE AXEL JUMP
The skater is attempting a double axel on the floor as part of the specific warm-up. Note the extension of the free leg, tight closed in-air rotation position, and excellent landing position on the floor.

DRYLAND PAIRS LIFT
A pair team performs a press lift as part of its specific pairs warm-up.

Warm-Up Activities for Ice Dance

Along with the specific exercises listed in Table 2.2, ice dancers would also use this time for specific off-ice warm-up of their dance lifts and/or choreography movements.

TABLE 2.2   ICE DANCE

Exercise	Sets	Repetitions	Rest Period
Ankle bounces[a]	3	8	1 minute
Double-leg diagonal quick jumps	3	8	1.5 minutes
Single-leg lateral stride jumps	3	6	2 minutes
Crossed-leg torso rotations[b]	3	10	30 seconds
Speed push-ups	2	5	1 minute
Dryland program run-throughs	—	—	—

a. See page 22.
b. See page 23.

DOUBLE-LEG DIAGONAL QUICK JUMPS
This ice dance skater is performing diagonal or zigzag double-leg jumps across the floor, emphasizing a quick accelerated takeoff, landing on the balls of the feet, and pushing through the floor with the ankles, legs, and arms. Note the correct positioning of the middle body.

SINGLE-LEG LATERAL STRIDE JUMPS
These photos show the sequence of single-leg lateral stride jumps across the floor. In this moderate-intensity drill, the skater initiates a power jump or stride off the single leg to the opposite side and then quickly pushes off the floor to jump back. Note the knee bend of the takeoff and landing leg.

SPEED PUSH-UPS
Push-ups are a specific warm-up exercise for the upper and middle body. Note the straight core or middle-body torso positioning and the depth of the push-up—the arms bent at a ninety-degree angle. The objective is to perform this exercise with a quick movement of the arms, up and down.

THE COOL-DOWN: RECOVERY OF THE SKATER

If a skater is not consistent about warming up and preparing for practice and competitive skating, then likely he or she is not doing an effective and appropriate cool-down. The cool-down is important for physical restoration or recovery after a practice session or competitive program. The cool-down can be very effective for the skater in the following ways:

- Reduce the amount of muscular soreness and/or tightness, especially in the legs and hip area

- Maintain, if not improve, flexibility

- Aid in the physical recovery process so that the skater is able to perform more efficiently throughout the week of training or at competitions

Guidelines for Cool-Down

1. Begin the cool-down active recovery immediately after practice or competitive program (within five minutes).

2. Perform the off-ice cool-down in a warm, dry environment (warm-up room or locker room).

3. Be sure to wear proper footwear.

4. Hold stretches for forty-five seconds to one minute; repeat stretches one to two times.

5. Drink plenty of fluids while performing the cool-down.

When should the skater perform the cool-down? The cool-down can be very effective in the following situations:

- Between on-ice practice sessions

- Immediately after the last practice session of the day

- During the week of a competition; this would take place immediately after each on-ice practice session

- Immediately after any competitive skating program (short or long)

- After off-ice strength/power and conditioning training

Physiologically speaking, the cool-down accomplishes two things: (1) It assists in blood flow, moving it away from the working muscles back to the heart or major organs of the middle body, and (2) it accelerates the removal of fatigue waste products (lactic acid) that accumulate during the training session or competitive program. It is well documented that skating a long program or back-to-back program run-throughs, performing a lot of technical jumps in a practice session, or even skating a short program may yield extremely high heart rates, expand the size of blood vessels, produce lactate, and thus, overall, increase neuromuscular and joint stress. Fatigue and exhaustion due to lactic acid accumulation can play a part in reducing a skater's ability to jump, spin, and perform sharp choreography, footwork, and arm movements and can affect judgment and concentration, increasing the potential for errors or missed elements. Cool-down exercises can help clear some of the accumulated lactic acid, thereby reducing fatigue, exhaustion, and stress. Performing light aerobic activity will allow oxygen to be processed, which will metabolize or clear the accumulated lactic acid. It is important to get the flow of blood back to the central organs—the heart and lungs—so that the blood does not pool or collect in the skater's legs.

ON-ICE STROKING FOR COOL-DOWN
This skater is performing on-ice moderate-paced stroking to cool down.

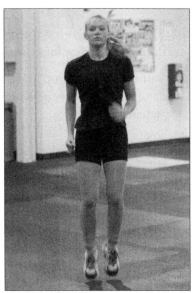

OFF-ICE COOL-DOWN
This skater is cooling down off-ice by executing light jogging in place.

FLEXIBILITY STRETCHING AS PART OF THE COOL-DOWN
This skater performs a partner-assisted supine knee flex. The off-ice coach is applying pressure against the skater's foot and leg to increase the skater's range of motion at the knee and hip joints to get a more efficient stretch. All total-body flexibility stretches should be performed as part of the cool-down stretch.

What does a skater need to do to cool down? A typical figure skater's cool-down routine involves active recovery, which uses aerobic activity for five to eight minutes to gradually reduce heart rate and get the blood moving back to the middle part of the body, followed by total-body flexibility stretching for at least fifteen minutes.

In active recovery, the skater may stroke on-ice for five minutes or more to gradually reduce heart rate. If ice time is a problem, the skater can change into his or her cross-training shoes and jog in place off-ice at a moderate pace for about five minutes. At competitions, the skater can stroke on-ice after practice sessions and the official warm-up. After the skater's short or initial program, he or she could cool down off-ice by jogging in place. A slideboard or stationary cycle is also good for active recovery. Following the active recovery, the skater should take his or her time and complete his or her total-body flexibility stretching.

Skaters can refer to the following checklist for warming up and cooling down. This checklist can be taken to the rink and used as a reminder or guideline for the warm-up and cool-down drill sequence.

Skater's Checklist for Off-Ice Warm-Up, Cool-Down, and Flexibility Stretching for Competition or Practice

NOTE: Perform off-ice warm-up at least forty-five minutes before getting your skates on and taking the ice for your on-ice warm-up. Use a soft landing surface and adequate footwear.

1. General Warm-Up (do one or more of the following for approximately five minutes)

   ___ jumping rope   ___ bench stepping   ___ footwork drills

   ___ jogging in place   ___ jogging stairs   ___ jumping jacks, calisthenics

2. Total-Body Flexibility Stretching (stretch once for each area and hold for twenty to thirty seconds; circle stretches: perform five each direction)

   ___ neck   ___ torso, lower back, abdominals   ___ hips

   ___ chest   ___ thighs, quadriceps (upper leg)   ___ calf (lower leg)

   ___ arms, shoulders, wrist   ___ hamstrings (upper leg)   ___ ankle, foot, shin

3. Specific Warm-Up Drills

   ___ jumps in place (double-leg equals ankle bounces with double-arm swings)

   ___ jumps for height and distance (double-leg equals lateral quarter squat jumps)

   ___ jumps for height (single-leg equals single-leg skip bounds)

   ___ torso/trunk rotations (crossed-leg position)

   ___ simulated axel/double axel takeoffs

   ___ floor landing position (check-outs)

   ___ jump landing check-outs

   ___ rotational jumps (double-leg to single-leg quarter air turns single, double, and triple jump rotations)

4. **Cool-Down**

____ gradually decrease heart rate by light- to moderate-paced stroking on-ice or jogging in place or using slideboard, or stationary cycle off-ice (approximately five minutes)

____ perform total-body flexibility stretches

CHAPTER 3

Strength Training for Figure Skating

trength is defined as the ability to produce or resist force. For the figure skater, strength is essential for stroking, spinning, and jumping, and for lifting a partner. Out of all the off-ice training components, strength training is the most important for continued success in skating. No matter what level of skating—preliminary to senior elite—strength training should be performed throughout a skater's entire career.[1] On-ice practice or skill work alone *will not* suffice for a complete total training of the skater. We know that strength training may be beneficial for injury prevention and enhanced skating performance. It increases the integrity or strength of the muscles, soft tissue, and bone so that the skater can better endure the stresses incurred from on-ice skill training.

For the elite skater, strength training may be the necessary tool to prolong his or her career. The elite skater may not have to jump higher, rotate faster, or lift his partner with greater strength; however, he needs to be concerned about being strong enough to *resist injury*, especially when that skater is traveling extensively for competitions. Skaters need a complete strength base to help prevent or reduce the rate of skating-related injuries.

And if a skater is injured, the strength-trained skater will recover more quickly. I have noticed that skaters I have strength-trained for longer than a year typically recover twice as fast from moderate injuries (such as strains, pulls, and impact-related injuries).

So what about strength training for the younger skater? Preliminary studies have looked at the forces involved in single, double, and triple rotational jumps.[2] Simply put, skaters endure a lot of stress at the ankle, knee, and hip joints and lower back while executing

DOUBLE AXEL LANDING
Note the excessive knee bend of the skater's landing leg. This photograph shows the great amount of stress that a skater endures on jump landing.

jumps. These impact stresses can be one to three times body weight on jump takeoff and three to nine times body weight on jump landing. Skaters of all levels must be physically strong enough to absorb the forces obtained from jump takeoffs and landings. Obviously, the higher the jump, the greater the impact stress when landing. Keep in mind how many times a skater will perform multirotational jumps on-ice during practice each day, accumulating each week, month, and year. This is an incredible volume of force that an immature, still-developing body encounters. To specifically calculate this for your skater, total the number of jump landings your skater attempts in a freestyle and multiply by 9, and then multiply that value by that skater's body weight. That total number is the amount of impact force in pounds of body weight that the bones, soft tissue, and muscles absorb on landing in one freestyle training (see below). Now relate this overall stress to the lower-level skater (preliminary, juvenile, intermediate) who is not yet fully grown.

EXAMPLE OF MAXIMUM FORCE OF JUMP LANDING STRESS

Skater body weight = 100 pounds

Total number of jumps per freestyle session = 20

Research value of stress = 9 × body weight

Equation = 9 × 100 pounds = 900 pounds

900 pounds × 20 jumps = 18,000 pounds of force

Strength-Training Instructor and Facility Guidelines

1. Instructor qualifications

   - Degree in exercise, physical education, or a sport science–related field (preferably master's degree)

   - Certification and membership through a professional association related to sports training (such as the National Strength and Conditioning Association or American College of Sports Medicine)

   - Membership through a professional association related to figure skating (such as the Professional Skaters Association or the United States Figure Skating Association)

   - Maintenance of continuing education credits within the instructor's specific professional association

   - Current working knowledge of the physiological and biomechanical characteristics, skills, and performances involved in various levels of skating; ability to perform an individual assessment of each skater

   - Knowledge of the concepts and principles involved in strength and conditioning training of the prepubescent athlete involving proper program design, exercise technique, safety, and spotting; program design and implementation should be individualized in many cases

   - Actual work experience hours (such as three to five hours) per week, training figure skaters off-ice

   - CPR certification (by the American Heart Association or Red Cross)

   - Ability to communicate well with the on-ice technical coach, physician, strength and conditioning coach, athletic trainer, and/or physical therapist

2. Strength- and conditioning training facility requirements

   - Adequate lighting and cleanliness

   - Adequate workout space and flooring with good traction and support

   - Proper equipment in good repair, including free weights and machines

3. Strength-training program design (specific to the individual athlete's age and abilities and figure skating)

(continued overleaf)

- Technique should be emphasized first, then progress to increased resistance

- Resistance (strength) training exercises should begin with high-volume, low-intensity (three to four sets of ten to fifteen repetitions) exercises

- Multijoint as well as isolated or single-joint exercises for the knees, hips, lower back, abdomen, shoulders, upper back, and ankles should be used

- Program design should vary, incorporating rest days and different exercises to prevent plateauing, monotony, and overtraining and to allow for peak levels of strength and power for the skater's performance

4. For the prepubescent skater (at any level of skating, preliminary to senior), strength-training program design and implementation must follow the guidelines of the "Position Statement: Youth Resistance Training," National Strength and Conditioning Association, 1996.[3]

Strength training can be extremely beneficial, productive, and safe for all levels of skaters (preliminary to senior elite). The following guidelines can help skaters, on-ice coaches, and parents find appropriate off-ice training for each skater.

STRENGTH-TRAINING PROGRAM DESIGN

For strength-training program design to be effective for the figure skater, we must perform the needs analysis of the skater described in detail in Chapter 1. Tables 3.1, 3.2, and 3.3 outline specific strength-training programs for all three disciplines of figure skating. These outlines are a good starting point for coaches and skaters to implement their off-ice strength training. Each outline takes into consideration the biomechanical movements on-ice and common sites of injury for all three disciplines. They can be used to perform specific exercises that incorporate movement patterns and muscle/joint areas specific to each discipline of skating. Also, the figure skater can identify the muscle/joint group or areas being trained. The outlines list the exercises in a specific order, with high-skill strength and power lifts first, then progressing to less technical movements. This exercise protocol is helpful for designing a training program.

Note: For instructional purposes, the skater should look at body positioning of the head, shoulders, chest, arms, torso, hips, knees, and feet in all the following photos of strength-training technique. This will help assist in correct exercise technique. Finally, the majority of these strength exercises should be performed in a slow/controlled movement, through a full range of motion. For ankle rocker exercise technique, refer to "Balance Training" in Chapter 4.

Strength Training for Singles

TABLE 3.1   STRENGTH-TRAINING EXERCISES FOR SINGLES

Exercise	*Area Trained*	*Specific Muscle Groups Trained*
Hang pull	Total body	Quadriceps, gluteals, hamstrings, spinal erectors, gastrocnemius, soleus, trapezius
Back squat	Lower body	Quadriceps, gluteals, hamstrings, spinal erectors
Bent-knee dead lift	Lower/ middle body	Hamstrings, gluteals, spinal erectors
Heel raises	Lower body	Gastrocnemius, soleus
Bench press	Upper body	Pectoralis major, triceps, deltoids
Push press (behind neck)	Total body	Quadriceps, gluteals, hamstrings, spinal erectors, gastrocnemius, soleus, deltoids, trapezius, triceps
Bent rows	Upper body	Latissimus dorsi, rhomboids, deltoids
Push-ups	Upper body	Pectoralis major, deltoids, triceps
Abdominal crunches	Middle body	Abdominals
Cycle crunches, leg-exchange crunches	Middle body	Obliques, abdominals
Ankle rocker balance	Lower body	Gastrocnemius, soleus, tibialis

HANG PULL
Start position. The hang pull begins with the arms extended holding the bar just above the knees; feet are approximately shoulder-width apart. Note the flat back and flexed hips and knees with the body weight over the middle portion of the feet. The torso is nearly erect; head is up.

Finish position. This photo shows the finish of the hang pull. Note the extension of the ankles, knees, and hips. The skater pulls the bar up with a jumping action and finishes with a shrug of the shoulders. Key points are to use the ankle, knee, and hip extensors to accelerate the bar vertically and keep it close to the midline of the body. Then return to the start position.

BACK SQUAT
Start position. Note that the skater has feet shoulder-width apart. The bar is placed just above the shoulder blades, hands are supporting the bar, and the head is up in a neutral position.

Low position. The skater flexes the hips and knees as if sitting back into a chair. Note that the torso is erect, back is flat, not rounded, feet are flat, and knees are aligned with the feet. The weight is over the middle of the feet or heels. The skater should lower until the top of the thighs are parallel to the floor, and then return to the start position. Always keep the eyes focused straight ahead.

BENT-KNEE DEAD LIFT
Start position. This start position is similar to the hang pull: chest is up, shoulders are square, and arms are relaxed and extended, holding the bar.

Middle position. Movement of the bar begins with flexing at the hips and waist and letting the bar travel down to just midway of the lower leg.

Low position. From the lowest position, the skater returns to the start position by extending the hips to bring the bar back to the start position. Torso needs to be erect; feet remain flat on the floor. Key point is to always maintain a flat back when performing the dead lift.

3 12

HEEL RAISES
Start position. The start position is very similar to the back squat, except that the balls of the feet are elevated on a block of wood.

Finish position. The skater has pushed up onto the toes, keeping the body in a vertical position. The heels should be raised in a slow, controlled manner, with the feet held in the raised position. The skater then lowers the heels back down to the floor.

Feet position for the beginning of the heel-raise strength exercise.

Note how the heels are lifted off the floor, the ankle is not "rolling out," and the range of motion is high up on the block of wood.

BENCH PRESS
Start position. With feet flat on the floor or bench, back flat on the bench, arms fully extended over the chest, and the bar held with a closed grip, this skater begins the bench press. The bench press requires a spotter.

Low position. Note that the skater has lowered the bar to just above the chest, while keeping the wrists straight, head stable, and feet flat on the floor or bench. By extending the elbow, the bar is pushed upward to the start position. This movement closely represents an arcing movement upward.

PUSH PRESS
Start position. The skater is in a start position similar to the back squat. Hands are shoulder-width apart, with fingers around the bar.

Middle position. In the drop phase of the lift, the skater lowers the bar similar to the quarter squat position with the torso erect and the hips and knees flexed. Immediately after getting to this position, the skater quickly begins the upward movement.

Finish position. For the upward movement to finish the lift, the skater explosively extends the knees and hips, and then extends the ankles, shifting the body weight toward the balls of the feet. At this point in the lift, the bar is pressed from the shoulders by extending the arms fully overhead. It is very important for the skater to keep the torso erect for core body stability. To return to the start position, the skater flexes at the hips and knees to lower the bar to the start position.

3 12

Finish position. With the torso erect and feet flat on the floor, the skater pulls the bar upward to the chest, making sure the elbows point up. Only the arms should move; the rest of the body needs to be firm for stability during the lift. To go back to the start position, the skater lowers the bar with control.

BENT ROWS
Start position. For bent rows, the skater starts with feet shoulder-width apart, knees slightly flexed, back flat, and head in a neutral position. The bar is held with arms fully extended; the bar does not touch the floor.

3 10

PUSH-UPS
Start position. Skater begins in a standard push-up position, with hands flat on the floor, arms fully extended, head in a neutral position, feet somewhat together, and the torso and hips in a straight line.

Low position. By flexing the elbows, the skater has lowered her body to the floor, while not touching the floor; arms should be at a ninety-degree angle. The skater returns to the start position by fully extending the arms to push the body upward. The key is to keep the middle body and lower back straight, not arched or rounded.

3 25

ABDOMINAL CRUNCHES
Start position. The skater is lying face up on the mat: back flat, knees bent, and hands behind the ears with elbows out.

Finish position. The skater curls her upper body toward the thighs, keeping feet flat and back pressed down on the mat. The skater must contract the abdominal muscles to initiate the upward movement and not pull on the head or upper body. Once up, the skater lowers her back to the mat to the start position.

3 30

CYCLE CRUNCHES
This dynamic abdominal/oblique strength exercise begins with the hips and knees at ninety-degree angles; the lower leg should be parallel to the floor. The rest of the body is in the same position as the abdominal crunches.

3 25

LEG-EXCHANGE CRUNCHES
Right leg. In this movement, the skater contracts the abdominals and side obliques to raise the upper body in a diagonal motion with the elbow meeting the knee of the opposite side.

Left leg. The skater brings the left knee to the right elbow. Remember to always move the elbow to the opposite knee, then switch sides. Care must be taken to keep the lower back firm against the mat, elbows out, and head in a somewhat neutral position.

Strength Training for Pairs

TABLE 3.2	STRENGTH-TRAINING EXERCISES FOR PAIRS	
Exercise	*Area Trained*	*Specific Muscle Groups Trained*
Hang high pull	Total body	Quadriceps, gluteals, hamstrings, gastrocnemius, soleus, spinal erectors, trapezius, deltoids, wrist flexors
Back squat[a]		
Bent-knee dead lift[b]		spinal erectors
Heel raise[c]		
Bench press[d]		
Front push press	Total body	Quadriceps, gluteals, hamstrings, gastrocnemius, soleus, spinal erectors, deltoids, trapezius, triceps, wrist flexors/ extensors
Bent rows[e]		
Close grip push-ups	Upper body	Pectoralis major, deltoids, triceps
Abdominal crunches[f]		Abdominals, obliques
Cycle crunches, leg-exchange crunches[g]		
Ankle rocker balance	Lower body	Gastrocnemius, soleus, tibialis

a. See page 40.
b. See page 40.
c. See page 41.
d. See page 42.
e. See page 43.
f. See page 44.
g. See page 44.

HANG HIGH PULL
Start position. The hang high pull begins with the same start position as the hang pull: arms extended and holding the bar just above the knees; feet are approximately shoulder-width apart. Note the flat back and flexed hips and knees with the body weight over the middle portion of the feet. Torso is nearly erect; head is up.

Middle position. This photo shows how the hang high pull differs from the hang pull. Note that as the skater extends the ankle, knee, and hip in a jumping motion, he explosively moves the bar up, close to the torso. As the bar reaches the top of the chest, the shoulders are shrugged and the arms flex and pull the bar to the top of the shoulders. Note in this photo how the skater's elbows move outward as the bar moves upward.

Finish position. The skater has reached the top of the pull. Note the complete vertical extension of the body; also the wrists are flexed and the skater continues to pull the bar to a high position. The bar movement stops at the neck, then the skater returns the bar to the start position, with knees and hips flexed and torso erect.

Close-up of the hand position for close-grip push-ups.

CLOSE-GRIP PUSH-UPS
Start position. The start position is similar to the standard push-up; however, the hands are placed close together on the floor, with the thumbs touching. Hands should be right under the chest, with torso straight.

Low position. Just as in the standard push-up, the skater has flexed at the elbow joint, lowering his body toward the floor, while keeping the hips, back, and upper body in a straight line. Skater extends the arms to go back to the start position.

FRONT PUSH PRESS
Start position. This strength/power exercise is very similar to the behind-the-neck push press, except the skater is gripping the bar in front of the body at shoulder height, with the elbows up. The bar is resting on the fingers and on the front of the shoulders.

Middle position. In the drop phase of the lift, the skater lowers the bar similar to the quarter squat position with the torso erect and the hips and knees flexed. Immediately after getting to this position, the skater quickly begins the upward movement.

Finish position. For the upward movement to finish the lift, the skater explosively extends the knees and hips, and then extends the ankles, shifting the body weight toward the balls of the feet. At this point in the lift, the bar is pressed from the shoulders by extending the arms fully overhead. It is very important for the skater to keep the torso erect for core body stability. To return to the start position, the skater flexes at the hips and knees to lower the bar to the start position.

Strength Training for Ice Dance

Keep in mind that for each listed exercise (such as the hang pull) there can be two or three similar or related exercises that can be periodized (see instructor and facility guidelines). The following detailed strength-training outline is only a sample start program. There can be variations in exercise type and order.

TABLE 3.3   STRENGTH-TRAINING EXERCISES FOR ICE DANCE

Exercise	Area Trained	Specific Muscle Groups Trained
Lunges	Lower body	Quadriceps, gluteals, hamstrings, spinal erectors
Bent-knee dead lift[a]		
Heel raises[b]		
Bench press[c]		
Front push press[d]	Total body	Quadriceps, gluteals, hamstrings, gastrocnemius, soleus, spinal erectors, deltoids, trapezius, triceps, wrist flexors/ extensors
Bent rows[e]		
Upright rows	Upper body	Trapezius, deltoids
Close-grip push-ups[f]		
Abdominal crunches[g]		Abdominals, obliques
Cycle crunches, leg-exchange crunches[h]		
Ankle rocker balance	Lower body	Gastrocnemius, soleus, tibialis

a. See page 40.
b. See page 41.
c. See page 42.
d. See page 47.
e. See page 43.
f. See page 46.
g. See page 44.
h. See page 44.

LUNGES
Start position. The start position is similar to the start position of the back squat. Feet are flat on the floor and shoulder-width apart; torso is erect, head in neutral position. The bar is resting just above the shoulder blades, with hands supporting the bar.

Middle position *(right leg)*. The skater has taken a step out with the right leg: the right foot is flat on the floor, the knee is over the middle to ball of the foot, and the top of the thigh is parallel to the floor. Make sure the torso is erect and straight; there should be no flexion of the back. After striding out, the skater will then push off the lead leg to return to the start position.

Middle position *(left leg)*. The skater is now striding out on the left leg. As the skater strides out, make certain the lead foot is flat on the floor and the knee does not go over the toes. Head is up and back/torso area remains erect and straight. Position is held, then the skater pushes back to the start position.

UPRIGHT ROWS
Start position. In the start position, the skater stands with feet shoulder-width apart and knees slightly bent. The torso is erect, and the bar is held with arms fully extended. The bar is gripped with hands about six to seven inches apart and fingers wrapped around the bar with a closed grip.

Middle position. The skater is pulling the bar upward along the abdomen and chest toward the chin; the elbows move outward during this phase of the lift.

Finish position. The lift is finished with the bar at the top of the chest. Note how the elbows are higher than the shoulders and are pointed out. The key is to keep the middle body erect and straight. Lower the bar under control back to the start position.

MAJOR AND ASSISTIVE STRENGTH EXERCISES

Major exercises are those strength and speed exercises that incorporate lifts with light, moderate, and some heavy resistance or loads, typically executed at a fast speed. Major exercises involve multijoint movements, using muscles that span more than one joint, thus controlling the movement of several body segments. These exercises have more carry-over to figure-skating movements due to their requirement of body alignment, control of multiple body segments, and high energy demand to actually perform the lift.

Assistive exercises are less technical, more isolated movements that typically involve a single phase or single-joint movement. These exercises build strength in specific areas for balance purposes. They are very important in strengthening the supportive muscles or joint areas used for the major lifts and strengthening the skater in specific areas for overall "total-body" physical preparation. These exercises typically require slower, more controlled movement patterns.

The following are suggested major and assistive strength-exercise choices for the sport of figure skating. Skaters can pair up or combine the following exercises from each category (1 through 10) to add to their strength workouts. Not all exercise categories have to be used (see Table 3.4). Pairs and ice dance skaters should add the assistive exercises in combinations for isolated strengthening of the arms, wrists, and leg adductors/abductors.

MAJOR

1. a. Hang pull
    b. Hang high pull   } Total body strength
    c. Hang clean
    d. Jump squats (lower body speed)

MAJOR

2. a. Back squat
    b. Front squat
    c. Lateral squat   } Lower body strength
    d. Single-leg squat
    e. Box step-ups
    f. Lutz (reverse) lunge

ASSISTIVE

3. a. Bent-knee dead lifts
    b. Back extensions   } Lower body strength
    c. Good mornings
    d. Dumbbell leg curls

ASSISTIVE

4. a. Heel raises
   b. In-out heel raises
   c. Single-leg heel raises
   d. Ankle rocker

} Lower body strength

MAJOR

5. a. Bench press
   b. Incline bench press
   c. Dumbbell bench press

} Upper body strength

MAJOR

6. a. Push press (behind neck)
   b. Front push press
   c. Drop push press
   d. Jerk press (landing position)

} Total body strength

ASSISTIVE

7. a. Bent rows
   b. Dumbbell bent rows
   c. One-arm rows
   d. Lat pull-down or seated rows

} Upper body strength

ASSISTIVE

8. a. Push-ups
   b. Pull-ups
   c. Bar dips
   d. Fit-ball push-ups

} Upper body strength

ASSISTIVE

9. a. Abdominal crunches
   b. Elevated crunches
   c. Fit-ball crunches
   d. Reverse crunches

10. a. Cycle crunches
    b. Oblique lateral crunches
    c. Fit-ball lateral crunch
    d. Fit-ball lateral twist

} Middle body strength

Tables 3.4 and 3.5 are examples of combining and varying more technical exercises for singles, pairs, and ice dance skaters, enabling them to progress to optimal strength/power production.

TABLE 3.4   COMBINATION OF MAJOR AND ASSISTIVE EXERCISES FOR SINGLES SKATERS

Exercise	Sets	Repetitions	Rest Period
Hang clean	3	5	2 minutes
Lateral squat	3	8	1 minute
Single-leg heel raise	3	6	1 minute
Jerk press	3	5	1.5 minutes
Fit-ball push-ups	3	8	1 minute
Fit-ball lateral twist	4	20	30 seconds

TABLE 3.5   COMBINATION OF MAJOR AND ASSISTIVE EXERCISES FOR PAIRS AND ICE DANCERS

Assistive Exercises	Major Exercises
Dumbbell triceps extension	Lunges
Dumbbell bicep curls	Lateral lunges
Wrist curl-ups	Box crossovers
Tennis ball (grip/squeeze)	Lateral squats
	Reverse lunges

The following strength-training logs can be used for skaters to fill out and chart their progression from workout to workout.

STRENGTH-TRAINING LOG

Name: _Kim-Bob Ruiz_   Height: _5'0_

Date: _____   Weight: _98_   Phase: _____

Time Period: _____

Program: _____   Rest Periods: _____   Warm-up: _____

Day: _____   Day: _____   Day: _____

Exercise	Sets	1	2	3	4
	wt.				
	reps.				
	wt.				
	reps.				
	wt.				
	reps.				
	wt.				
	reps.				
	wt.				
	reps.				
	wt.				
	reps.				
	wt.				
	reps.				

Exercise	Sets	1	2	3	4
	wt.				
	reps.				
	wt.				
	reps.				
	wt.				
	reps.				
	wt.				
	reps.				
	wt.				
	reps.				
	wt.				
	reps.				
	wt.				
	reps.				

Exercise	Sets	1	2	3	4
	wt.				
	reps.				
	wt.				
	reps.				
	wt.				
	reps.				
	wt.				
	reps.				
	wt.				
	reps.				
	wt.				
	reps.				
	wt.				
	reps.				

Intensity of workout: _____

How did you feel?_____

_____

STRENGTH-TRAINING LOG

Name: _____ Program: **Singles** Rest Periods: _____ Warm-Up: _____ Phase: _____

Start Date: _____

bwt = body weight as resistance

Exercise	sets	1/1	1/2	1/3	1/4																			
Hang Pulls	lbs.																							
	reps.	10	10	10																				
Back Squats	lbs.																							
	reps.	12	12	12																				
Bent-Knee Dead-Lifts	lbs.																							
	reps.	12	12	12																				
Heel Raises	lbs.																							
	reps.	12	12	12																				
Bench Press	lbs.																							
	reps.	12	12	12																				
Push Press	lbs.																							
	reps.	12	12	12																				
Bent Rows	lbs.																							
	reps.	8	8	8																				
Push-Ups	lbs.	bwt	bwt	bwt																				
	reps.	5–10	5–10	5–10																				
Abdominal Crunches	lbs.	bwt	bwt	bwt																				
	reps.	10–25	10–25	10–25																				
Cycle Crunches	lbs.	bwt	bwt	bwt																				
	reps.	10–30	10–30	10–30																				
Ankle Rocker	lbs.	bwt	bwt	bwt																				
	reps.	10	10	10																				
Stretching: Total Body	duration																							
	reps.																							
How do you feel?																								
Intensity of Workout																								

STRENGTH-TRAINING LOG

Name: _____ Program: _____ Rest Periods: _____ Warm-Up: _____ Phase: _____

Start Date: _____

bwt = body weight as resistance

Pairs

Exercise	sets	1/1	1/2	1/3	1/4																			
Hang High Pulls	lbs.																							
	reps.	8	8	8																				
Back Squats	lbs.																							
	reps.	12	12	12																				
Bent-Knee Dead-Lifts	lbs.																							
	reps.	12	12	12																				
Heel Raises	lbs.																							
	reps.	12	12	12																				
Bench Press	lbs.																							
	reps.	12	12	12																				
Front Push Press	lbs.																							
	reps.	8	8	8																				
Bent Rows	lbs.																							
	reps.	12	12	12																				
Close-Grip Push-Ups	lbs.	bwt	bwt	bwt																				
	reps.	5–10	5–10	5–10																				
Abdominal Crunches	lbs.	bwt	bwt	bwt																				
	reps.	10–25	10–25	10–25																				
Cycle Crunches	lbs.	bwt	bwt	bwt																				
	reps.	10–30	10–30	10–30																				
Ankle Rocker	lbs.	bwt	bwt	bwt																				
	reps.	10	10	10																				
Stretching: Total Body	duration																							
	reps.																							

How do you feel?

Intensity of Workout

STRENGTH-TRAINING LOG

Name: _____ Program: _____ Rest Periods: _____ Warm-Up: _____ Phase: _____

Start Date: _____ **Ice Dance**

bwt = body weight as resistance

Exercise	sets	1/1	1/2	1/3	1/4
Lunges	lbs.				
	reps.	12	12	12	12
Bent-Knee Dead-Lifts	lbs.				
	reps.	12	12	12	12
Heel Raises	lbs.				
	reps.	12	12	12	12
Bench Press	lbs.				
	reps.	12	12	12	12
Front Push Press	lbs.				
	reps.	8	8	8	8
Bent Rows	lbs.				
	reps.	12	12	12	12
Upright Rows	lbs.				
	reps.	12	12	12	12
Close-Grip Push-Ups	lbs.	bwt	bwt	bwt	bwt
	reps.	5–10	5–10	5–10	5–10
Abdominal Crunches	lbs.	bwt	bwt	bwt	bwt
	reps.	10–25	10–25	10–25	10–25
Cycle Crunches	lbs.	bwt	bwt	bwt	bwt
	reps.	10–30	10–30	10–30	10–30
Ankle Rocker	lbs.	bwt	bwt	bwt	bwt
	reps.	10	10	10	10
Stretching: Total Body	duration				
	reps.				

How do you feel?

Intensity of Workout

PRINCIPLES FOR OFF-ICE STRENGTH TRAINING

Once a coach knows what exercises to use, the next step is structuring the strength training. For any strength program to be successful, the following variables need to be understood and utilized.

1. Frequency. Strength training should be performed at least two to three times per week.
2. Duration. Length of actual strength-training workouts should be approximately forty-five to fifty minutes.
3. Volume. Skaters should generally perform three to four sets of eight to twelve repetitions per exercise. *Note:* Abdominal/oblique or torso exercises can have higher repetitions of fifteen to twenty per set, per exercise.
4. Intensity. Also known as training load, this reflects the amount of weight lifted per repetition, or repetition maximum (RM). Skaters should perform exercises 8 RM to 12 RM. In other words, the training load or amount of weight selected for a skater should allow him or her to perform 8 RM to 12 RM per set with correct exercise technique.
5. Rest. Rest or recovery should last approximately one to two minutes between sets and exercises. Abdominal/oblique or core body exercises can have a rest period of thirty to forty-five seconds. Recovery between strength workouts should be at least twenty-four hours.
6. Exercise type. Perform total-body strengthening exercises, biomechanically specific to the muscle/joint areas and movement patterns utilized in figure skating skill movements (such as the exercises listed in the outline). Also, perform assistive exercises (isolated movements) for areas of possible muscular imbalance for injury prevention.
7. Order of exercise. Perform multijoint or total-body technical exercises first, then progress to the less technical (isolated) movements; for example, perform back squats before heel raises.

Of all the principles, the most important variable for proper strength progression of the skater is exercise intensity. However, strength-training intensity can also be the most detrimental to strength performances. For a joint structure, such as the knee joint, to increase in strength, there must be a progressive overload or increase in resistance to that particular area. For instance, if a skater begins a back squat with fifteen pounds of resistance, three sets of ten repetitions, after a couple of strength-training workouts, he or she may increase the back squat to twenty pounds at three sets of ten repetitions. The most common way to enhance strength gains is the overload principle, or progressively increasing resistance to the working musculature area. However, care needs to be taken, especially for the younger skater or the skater that does not need a large increase in muscular mass, not to make a large increase in resistance. To keep it simple, skaters can safely and effectively increase lifting resistance approximately five to ten pounds per exercise for an appropriate overload, or increase resistance 5 to 10 percent. These increases may occur after every other workout, weekly, or every other week over the course of a six- to eight-week strength-training cycle.

Rate of increase depends on proper technique and adaptation of the skater. Progressive overload can be individualized to each skater, depending on his or her technical potential.

Eventually, the skater will reach a plateau in exercise resistances. This may be a good time to modify the skater's strength program by changing to different exercises. There can also be variation with the number of sets, repetitions, and rest periods.

Basic Guidelines for Off-Ice Strength Training

1. Perform a brief warm-up with total-body flexibility stretches before strength workouts. Skaters do not need to warm up if they are performing their off-ice workout immediately after skating.

2. The workout should be a combination of free weights (barbells and dumbbells), exercise machines (such as the lat pull-down and leg curl machines), and using the skater's own body weight for resistance. Keep in mind that free weights and body-weight exercise drills are superior for strength training. Sport cords are used for more skating-specific speed and strength movements (see Chapter 4).

3. Loads or the total amount of resistance lifted must be adjusted for the age, strength, and technical ability of the skater. Always emphasize proper technique first, and then increase resistance. Overall, skaters should do three to four sets of eight to twelve repetitions.

4. Proper technique should always be emphasized. Part of proper technique includes the following:

   - A controlled, moderate speed of lifting movement

   - Good body form

   - Correct body alignment or positioning

   - Breathing while lifting

   - Constant communication or feedback regarding all exercises

5. Safety of strength training is a requirement. Safety issues include the following:

   - Skaters involved in any type of off-ice strength training should be instructed by qualified personnel. This is especially true for the prepubescent skater.

   - Use spotters for strength exercises (such as back squat, push press, and bench press). Spotters are needed to assist the skater in executing the exercise and in using proper technique and to motivate him or her.

- The off-ice training facility, whether a weight room, fitness center, or gym, should have lots of space and safe exercise equipment. The skater should wear proper footwear and clothing.

- Program variation is a must for safety and progression. If a skater is injured or overly fatigued, individualize or modify the workout to meet his or her needs. For example, if a skater is fatigued from a lot of program run-throughs or jumps, the volume and intensity of his or her strength workout should be reduced (fewer sets and repetitions or less resistance). Or, change the exercise selection to concentrate on a body area or movement pattern that is not fatigued from on-ice practice.

- During off-ice training, skaters should concentrate while performing exercises and assist and encourage each other. If a skater is concerned about lifting technique or needs spotting, he or she should ask for help. Not concentrating on proper technique can result in serious injury. I witnessed one skater talking to another skater while executing an exercise, and as a result, she tripped on a plyometric box and fell to the floor. Although this accident wasn't serious, it highlights the importance of maintaining concentration while performing an exercise.

CHAPTER 4

Off-Ice Jump Training, Sport Cord Speed Drills, and Balance Training

Once a certain degree of leg, hip, core, and upper body strength is established, I feel it is important to cycle in off-ice jump training. In general terms, off-ice jump training is a way to integrate the fundamentals of strength and speed, body awareness, coordination, or overall body control. These general exercises teach skaters how to jump in place on the floor, using the total body with good technique. Skaters spend so much time in constrictive skating boots, they do not know how to use the muscles of the lower leg to jump, so it is important to teach this skill. At the same time, and also throughout some of the strength training, balance training should be implemented. It is important for the skater to use balance training to further develop his or her fine motor skills; plus, this training also strengthens the lower leg, foot, and ankle. Good balance requires complete control of the body. Skaters must balance dynamically or work on balance movements. Some of the jump-training drills definitely help develop dynamic balance.

One of the fundamental on-ice skill movements that I include in off-ice training is jump rotations. Skaters, off-ice strength coaches, trainers, and on-ice coaches should have a common objective to make training as specific as possible to the movement performed on-ice. In an effort to train specific strength/power movement patterns instead of just training muscle groups, I have incorporated dryland rotational jump drills into the off-ice program, as well as weight and sport cord drills. These drills simulate as closely as possible the jump rotation and landing position of on-ice jumps. Although using the blade for takeoff and for gliding on the ice after landing can't be simulated, these dry-land rotational jumps are extremely important for improving the following:

1. Body control and body awareness
2. Takeoff power (the initial strength and speed that the skater attains during jump takeoffs and leg, hip, torso, and arm movement)
3. Rotational speed and quickness (speed of obtaining a tight in-air body position)
4. Landing control and strength

Using dryland rotational jumps for supplemental training has unique advantages:

1. It's inexpensive; skaters can work on rotations on the ground or floor, without the cost of ice.
2. It's less stressful to the body (no falling down on-ice, no stress from the boots).
3. Skaters can work on rotations more frequently.

DRYLAND DOUBLE AXEL
Skater is attempting a double axel on the floor. Note the power and control going into the jump.

How often or when should skaters perform dryland rotational jumps? Skaters can incorporate jump rotations in the following situations:

1. Off-ice warm-up preparation
2. Strength-training workouts
3. Plyometric-training workouts
4. Tactical/circuit conditioning drill sequences

In a strength workout, at the end of the workout (usually after the torso/abdominal exercises), skaters can go through a portion of their dryland rotations and then perform their total-body flexibility stretching. During a plyometric workout (see Chapter 5), skaters can perform their dryland rotations at the beginning of the workout. This is a beneficial sequence because the rotations are a good warm-up for the more demanding plyometric drills that follow.

Establishing proper safety and technique guidelines is very important before starting a jump-training program. The following guidelines should be followed to maximize and safely execute off-ice dryland rotational drills.

Safety Guidelines for Off-Ice Jump Training

1. Select an appropriate instructor for program design and supervising training sessions.

2. Incorporate proper skill development or progression. Skaters should mainly work on dryland jumps (singles, doubles, or triples) appropriate to their skill level for their on-ice jumps. If a skater is not training or attempting triple jumps on-ice, then he or she should emphasize appropriate technique for only double jumps off-ice.

3. Proper equipment use:

   • Footwear should have adequate heel/ankle support (cross-trainer or basketball shoe).

   • Jumps should be performed on a soft, nonskid landing surface (mats, cushioned aerobic floor, or sprung ballet floor). The surface should be resilient enough to reduce some of the landing stress; however, it should not be so thick that it impedes jump takeoff.

4. Engage in strength training before and throughout the off-ice jump training to develop an adequate strength base.

5. Emphasize the following techniques:

   • Explosive power on jump takeoff (forceful push off the floor); good knee, hip, and ankle flexion and extension

   • Explosive and quick use of the arms for pulling in

   • Closed (tight) lower and upper body positioning on the vertical axis of rotation; overall, quick rotation speed

   • Correct postural alignment: head straight and up, shoulders square, torso straight

   • Controlled landing position: a good eccentric knee bend on the landing leg, landing on the ball of the foot, complete arm extension, shoulders square, head and arms up

   • Free leg extending out as quickly as possible on landing; skater should hold the landing position for at least a two-second count

6. Vary the program for both safety of the jump drill and also to progress with jump/skill acquisition. Program variables that can be changed are:

(continued overleaf)

- Type of jumps (toe loop, loop, flip, lutz, and axel)

- Intensity of jump (single, double, triple) or using external resistance (weight belt or vest)

- Volume (sets and repetitions, which equal the total number of attempted jump takeoffs and landings)

- Rest (recovery time between sets and/or jump types)

- Frequency (number of jump workouts or training sessions per week, such as two to three times per week)

Note: As with strength training, care should be taken to manipulate or vary off-ice jump training. Various factors such as fatigue, skater's skill potential, and total volume of jumps should be considered. Off-ice jumping should not be high-volume training.

JUMP-TRAINING INTENSITY PROGRESSION

A program variable important not only for strength training but also for dryland jump training is increasing the intensity of training using external resistance. I have skaters wear or hold weights while they perform their rotational jumps. Three specific methods of using external resistance are:

1. Ankle weights. These weights wrap around the lower leg or ankle area. They can range from one-quarter pound to five pounds each.
2. Weight belt or vest. The belt or vest is worn around the waist or chest area of the skater. These can range from one-quarter pound to fifteen pounds.
3. Handheld dumbbells. These weights are used for upper body drills. They can range from one pound to ten pounds.

Why should skaters increase intensity or use external resistance? Skaters can advance at an accelerated rate with dryland rotational jumps. It is important to use added resistance with skaters who need an extra challenge or who require more upper and/or lower body explosiveness. Skaters have indicated that the weight belt or vest makes them use their arms and upper bodies more. Another advantage is that ankle weights simulate the weight of the boots and blades while a skater performs his or her rotations. Care should be taken when using external weights with skaters. The intensity should reflect the age, level, and ability of the skater. You can obtain excellent results from ankle weights of two to three pounds for juvenile- through novice-level skaters and use of a weight belt of up to five pounds for novice- to senior-level skaters. Overall, these variables *need to be individualized and periodized.* External resistance dryland jump training should only be implemented with

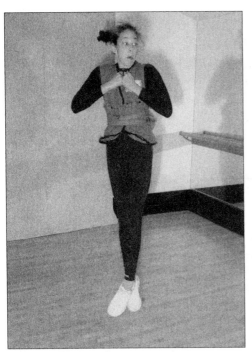

DRYLAND DOUBLE JUMP ATTEMPT WITH WEIGHT VEST
The skater is attempting a double-loop jump with a weight vest to add an overload resistance to the jump. The vest does not affect jump technique of the legs, hips, and arms because it conforms to the chest and upper back.

the skater who has an adequate strength base and is proficient in performing jump rotations on the floor.

This training can have the following benefits: increased leg and arm power, tighter air position, and especially quicker check-out of the jump, getting into landing position. Check-out, or deceleration of jump rotation, involves arm extension, free-leg extension, and a significant knee bend of the landing leg. (See Chapter 5 for an example of a drill log for off-ice dryland jump rotations.)

WATER AND SPORT CORD TRAINING

Water Training

I use two other modes for training jumps off-ice: water and sport cord training. I have used water (a lap swimming pool) for training rotational jumps and jump drills for skating-related movements. Skaters can train in water by simulating similar jump movements in waist-deep water. Technique should emphasize quick explosive movement, similar to any dryland drill. Such drills as ankle bounces, tuck jumps, and skipping can all be performed in the water. Also, rotational jumps can be simulated with the water providing the resistance. Water training has the following benefits:

1. It adds external resistance with minimal stress to the joints when performing the drills.
2. It is an excellent method for allowing a skater recovering from injury to train without much stress to the body.
3. It is a good way for adding variation (periodization) to a skater's off-ice training, which helps avoid monotony.

As far as the program design for jump training in water, try to be specific and creative using the variables of frequency, volume, intensity, and rest periods. Overall, the water can provide an excellent method for training jumps such as the loop, flip, and lutz (which are all easy to simulate on the floor) and for takeoff drills for the axel. Ice dancers can use the water for lateral power drills, such as lateral stride jumps, which focus on horizontal distance, and for reinforcing stroking movements.

65

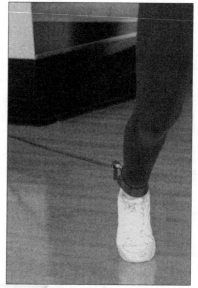

**SKATER POSITIONING AND
SPORT CORD ATTACHMENT**
The sport cord is around the skater's
ankle and attached to the door: the
skater is now ready to perform the drill
sequences. Care should be taken to
make sure the cord is attached securely
to the door and on the same level as the
skater's ankle.

Here you can see a close-up of the cord
attached around the skater's ankle.

Sport Cord Training

I use sport cords as part of warm-up drills before rotational jump training or plyometrics and after strength workouts for the preliminary- through intermediate-level skater. Sport cords are good for training quickness (speed/strength), power, and balance of skill components. The drills are effective for training the following:

- Axel and double axel takeoff (free leg going through)

- Landing position with free-leg extension (from a crossed-leg closed position)

- Free-leg pull-through

- Arm extensions (simulation of arm extending to the check-out position)

The sport cord is similar to surgical tubing with varying degrees of tensile (tension) strength. Sport cord colors reflect the tension or strength of the cord. For stronger cords, the thickness and color of the cord will vary. The cords are attached just above the ankle.

PARTNER-HELD SPORT CORD SETUP
Here, the off-ice coach is assisting with the exercise drills by holding the sport cord for the skater. The key is to hold the cord firmly at the level of the skater's ankle, not to pull it.

The other end of the cord can be held by a partner, or the skater can use the cord alone by attaching it to a doorway or around a piece of stable exercise equipment.

The following are some guidelines for using sport cords:

1. Perform three to four sets of eight to ten repetitions per drill.
2. Emphasize quickness of the leg and/or arm segments that you are training.
3. Make certain the skater has correct posture or body alignment of the head, shoulders, torso, knee, and foot on the landing-leg side.
4. Skaters should use their upper bodies and arms in sequence with their lower bodies. To get creative, add handheld dumbbells or wrist weights for the upper body and arms.
5. Position the skater's body as specifically as possible for both takeoff and landing drills (as it would be on the ice). Monitor upper, middle, and lower body positioning and angle of free-leg movement.

Sport cord exercises may also be performed with ankle and wrist weights as resistance loads. Load ranges or intensity would be determined by the age, level, technical ability, and strength base of the skater. Typically, skaters use one to five pounds of resistance. Table 4.1 shows a sport cord training program.

CORD: SPEED/RESISTANCE TRAINING PROGRAM

	Sets	Repetitions	Cord Color	Rest Period
	3	10	Green	30 seconds–1 minute
	3	10	Green	30 seconds–1 minute
In-air rotation position; landing position check-outs	3	10	Green	30 seconds–1 minute
Arm-extension check-outs or 3-pound dumbbell	3	10	Green	30 seconds–1 minute

AXEL/DOUBLE AXEL TAKEOFFS
Start position. The skater is positioned with the sport cord in an axel takeoff position. The skater has stepped out to make the cord tight. Shoulders are square and head is up. Note the knee bend in the takeoff leg and the arms held back.

Finish position. The skater has stepped up through the takeoff, up on the ball of the foot of the takeoff leg, with arms extending through the takeoff. Note the cord attached to the free leg, which is extending through the takeoff; this is where the resistance is applied. The skater then relaxes and steps back into the start position for another repetition.

LEG PULL-THROUGH
Start position. The cord is attached to the left leg. The skater has stepped back to keep the cord tight; left leg is extended, arms are up, and head is neutral. The skater is in a position similar to a loop takeoff.

Finish position. The skater has, as quickly as possible, pulled the left leg (cord leg) into a closed in-air rotation position and has simultaneously pulled the arms into the midline of the body. The skater then slowly returns the free leg to the start position.

IN-AIR ROTATION POSITION
WITH CHECK-OUT
Start position. Here the skater is simulating an in-air rotation position while standing on the floor. The cord is attached to the free leg and stretched out. Ankles are together, arms tight, torso erect, and head in a neutral position.

Finish position. The skater is in the checked-out position: the cord is tight, free leg is high, arms are up and extended, shoulders are square, torso is erect, and head is stabilized. This movement should be performed as quickly as possible. After holding the landing position for a slow two-second count, the skater then returns to the start position.

This close-up photo shows how the skater is holding the sport cord, prior to checking out or extending the arms.

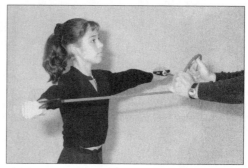

ARM CHECK-OUTS WITH SPORT CORD
Start position. The skater is in a closed-arm position, holding the sport cord, while a partner holds the other end of the cord. Make sure the skater is standing tall, elbows are in tight, head is stable, and there is some resistance with the cord.

Finish position. As quickly as possible, the skater has checked out the arms (complete arm extension); the arms are held high with no bend in the elbow. Head is up and stable. This movement can be done in conjunction with the in-air position leg check-outs.

ARM CHECK-OUTS WITH DUMBBELLS
Start position. The skater is perfoming the same movement as the sport cord arm check-out, except the skater is holding dumbbells in the closed-arm position. These dumbells can range in weight from one to ten pounds, depending upon the base strength of the skater.

Finish position. Skater has checked out the arms, extending the dumbbells outward. Again, the skater needs to hold the extended position for a slow two-second count before returning to the start position.

BALANCE TRAINING

Training for balance is very important for the preliminary- to inte
Off-ice work on motor skills and coordination for young skaters ma
skill acquisition, especially edge control and the overall control of la

Performing drills on an ankle rocker is an effective method for
ankle rocker is a metal device that creates an unstable surface. It is place
provides a rocking-type movement in one direction.

Ankle rocker balance/speed drills can help the skater in the following ways:

1. Strengthen and increase flexibility of the foot and ankle or lower leg (calf)
2. Train balance properties and enhance body awareness
3. Train various skating skill movements while working on balance and coordination and combining speed and balance
4. Add variation to the overall off-ice program or periodization

Body positioning should be emphasized; the skater should simulate on the ankle rocker the exact on-ice body position. Once good technique is achieved, the skater should try some of the more dynamic skill movements with quick speed of movement. Table 4.2 shows just a few of the skills that can be performed. You can get quite creative with other drills on the ankle rocker as well as with the sport cords.

TABLE 4.2   ANKLE ROCKER BALANCE/SPEED DRILLS

Exercise	*Volume (sets × repetitions)*	*Rest Period*
Ankle rocker flexion/ eversion and inversion	3 × 10	1 minute
Balance holds, single leg	10 seconds–1 minute	1 minute
Axel takeoffs	3 × 8	30 seconds–1 minute
Landing check-outs	3 × 8	30 seconds–1 minute
Camel and spiral positions	10 seconds–1 minute	1 minute

Note: Drills 1, 2, and 5 should be performed on both legs and feet.

ANKLE ROCKER
The ankle rocker device is used for balance, flexibility, and strengthening of the ankle/foot or lower leg area.

**ANKLE ROCKER FLEXION/
FOOT POSITIONING**
This photo shows the skater in plantar flexion of the foot on the ankle rocker. The foot presses on the ankle rocker; as the foot rocks upward, the heel lifts off the floor. This movement should first be performed in a slow, controlled manner, then speed can be added. The skater can support himself or herself by holding onto a wall or perform this freestanding with total balance. The free leg should remain off the floor for balance and to make the drill more technical.

**BODY POSITIONING ON
THE ANKLE ROCKER**
The skater stands tall with one foot on the ankle rocker; head should be up and the ball of the foot positioned on the ankle rocker.

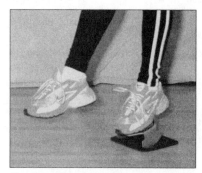

Here is a close-up of the movement at the ankle area. Note the foot positioning on the ankle rocker.

ANKLE ROCKER EVERSION
Here the skater positions the ankle rocker at a diagonal position; the ball of the foot is placed on the rocker. The movement should be in one direction, with the ankle/foot moving outward or toward the outside of the foot. As the foot rotates down and out, the skater then presses back up to the start position, with the top of the foot parallel to the floor.

ANKLE ROCKER INVERSION
This uses the same foot position as the eversion drill; however, instead of going out with the foot, the skater moves the foot down and in by pressing or pushing, and then returns to the start position, with the foot parallel to the floor.

SINGLE-LEG BALANCE HOLDS
This is a great drill for training balance on one leg. Note that the skater is positioned freestanding on the ankle rocker. This is a total balance drill as the skater has no contact with the free leg to the floor or opposite leg and no contact of the arms with a wall. The skater holds the balanced position for a designated time. Note: for good control, it is recommended that the free leg remain stable, the arms held up and out, and the head up and stable. This is also a performance test (see Chapter 7).

ANKLE ROCKER AXEL TAKEOFFS
Start position. The skater is in an axel takeoff position on the ankle rocker. Note the positioning of the takeoff leg, and the reach back of the arms, and the free leg.

Finish position. This photo shows the finished position of the axel takeoff. Note the free leg coming through, and more important, the action of the arms and takeoff leg, with the skater rocking up on the toe of the takeoff leg. The goal is to perform this exercise with the same speed of movement as the axel on the ice. This is a great speed/balance drill simulating the jump takeoff action of the axel.

**ANKLE ROCKER LANDING/
CHECK-OUT**
Start position. The skater is positioned in an in-air rotation position while the landing leg is on the ankle rocker instead of the floor. Note the ankles are crossed, arms in tight, and good posture.

Finish position. As quickly as possible, the skater has checked out, while keeping the landing foot (right foot) secured on the ankle rocker. Note the good extension of the free leg and arms. The torso is erect, shoulders square, and head stable. The key is to perform this drill with good speed, but to hold the check-out position (balanced on the ankle rocker) for a slow two-second count.

**ANKLE ROCKER CAMEL
AND SPIRAL POSITIONS**
The ankle rocker is an excellent device to simulate camel/spiral positions. Here the skater is attempting a spiral position while balanced on the ankle rocker. The objective is to maintain the correct position for a designated time. Note the extended free leg, arm extension, and low back positioning.

CHAPTER 5

Plyometric Training for Figure Skating

Plyometric training suddenly increased in popularity in off-ice training for figure skaters. However, I have observed skaters performing plyometric drills that have been more of a risk than a benefit to the skater. Just like strength training, plyometrics can be very effective for the skater (increasing lower, middle, and upper body power, stability, body awareness, and balance properties); however, plyometrics can be extremely detrimental to the skater's body, especially the prepubescent skater. Coaches that allow their skaters to perform plyometrics should be aware of these concerns.

Plyometrics involve jumping drills, torso and abdominal drills and upper body drills, to train the neuromuscular system. The skater uses drill technique to produce a quick, forceful, dynamic movement. The overall objective is to make a forceful muscular contraction or movement as quickly as possible. The skater is training his or her muscles (joint areas) to contract as quickly as possible with the highest amount of force possible. Specific to figure skating, plyometrics may be effective for the following:[1]

SINGLES

1. Increasing stroking power
2. Increasing jump height
3. Increasing rotation speed
4. Increasing landing strength (enhancing the eccentric or muscle-lengthening component)

PAIRS

1. All of the above (singles)
2. Increasing height of pairs lifts and power for throw jumps
3. Increasing core stability for pairs lifts

ICE DANCE

1. Increasing stroking power
2. Increasing power of dance lifts
3. Increasing core stability for dance movements

Similar to strength training, the main emphasis with plyometrics should be on technique, proper progression, and safety. However, plyometrics stresses the body, especially at the following joint areas: ankle, knee, hip and lower back, shoulder, elbow, wrist, and neck. Anytime a skater adds supplemental off-ice plyometric training, care should be taken to monitor the volume (sets and repetitions or foot contacts) and intensity (double-leg or single-leg jumps, varying box heights, or amplitude or type of drill). I try to monitor a skater's accumulative number of jumps on-ice, especially when he or she is in a plyometric training phase.

Skaters perform a kind of plyometric activity on-ice. For instance, when a singles skater performs a combination jump, the landing (unloading) and takeoff (loading) reflects the eccentric to concentric neuromuscular (nervous system stimulus to muscular contraction) action of the leg, hip, and ankle structures. One can see this as the skater comes out of the rotation of the first jump and quickly accelerates into the second part of the jump combination. These jump combinations are a form of plyometrics training on-ice. It is important to train the speed of jump takeoffs and especially the strength (eccentrics) of landings. Overall, plyometric training for the singles skater may enhance leg and hip power for increased jump height and torso rotation power for strength of rotation.

Pairs skaters closely simulate plyometric activity with their jumps, in particular stressing the torso and lower back and shoulder joints during their lifts and throw jumps. Ice dancers perform the same movements with their lifts and also with their dynamic stroking maneuvers. Overall, one can see how skaters in all three disciplines go through the neuromuscular action just by performing their typical on-ice movements. Thus, when skaters combine their on-ice practice sessions with supplemental plyometric training, this can increase the frequency, volume, and possibly the intensity of training, creating even more stress to joint areas and possibly increasing mental fatigue.

It is very important for skaters and coaches, both off-ice and on-ice, to communicate and monitor the skater's volume and intensity of training, or training load. For instance, if a skater has just performed three practice sessions with a lot of dynamic technical work (jumps, lifts, stroking) or program run-throughs, his or her off-ice training should be *modified*, especially if it is a planned plyometric session. Thus, under these conditions the actual plyometric drill protocol would be low intensity and low volume with longer rest periods. For example, instead of performing planned single-leg jumps, the skater might perform double-leg jump drills with fewer foot contacts and rest for extended periods, possibly up to three to four minutes.

Guidelines for plyometric training are similar to strength training with some modifications. Skaters should adhere to the following guidelines for proper execution of and safety during plyometric training. Sample plyometric training drill sheets can be found on pages 81, 86, and 88. Training logs to chart progress can be found on pages 90–92.

Plyometric Training Guidelines

Program Design

1. Plyometric drills need to be designed to be appropriate to the age, level, and ability of the skater.

2. Periodization of the plyometric program design variables (volume, intensity, rest, recovery, frequency, and variation of prescribed exercises) should be used to prevent overtraining.

    - Volume. Total number of foot contacts (number of repetitions times number of sets).

    - Intensity. Measured by the height and distance (amplitude) of the drill or type of drills performed (example: double-leg or single-leg drills, ten-inch box or eighteen-inch box).

    - Drills/exercises. Variation of drills is important for plyometric drill or skill acquisition and to prevent or overcome plateaus.

    - Rest. Determined by the intensity of the drill: one-minute rest for jumps in place (low-intensity drill); two- to three-minute rest for box jumps (high-intensity drill).

    - Recovery. Amount of time between jump/plyometric drill sessions; at least forty-eight hours of recovery time is appropriate.

    - Frequency. Plyometric sessions should only be performed one to two times per week.

3. A strength-training phase of at least eight to ten weeks should be implemented before starting any plyometric training for developing a total-body strength base. The skater needs to become stronger to benefit from plyometrics without risk of injury.

4. Drills should progress from general motor skill development to skating-specific skills, especially in preparing for the competitive season. Cycles or training phases should be appropriate to the competitive season; for

(continued overleaf)

example, progressing from double-leg jumps off-season to single-leg jumps during preseason and in-season.

5. The skater needs the proper equipment and training facility.

- Footwear. Shoes with appropriate ankle/heel support (basketball, volleyball, or cross-training shoes).

- Facility. A soft, absorbing landing surface with appropriate space should be utilized (aerobics floor, mats, sprung wooden floor, or soft grass).

- Accessory equipment:

  Boxes. Jump boxes should be durable (¾-inch thick plywood) with at least an 18- by 24-inch nonskid landing surface. Box heights can range from 6 to 8 inches up to 14 inches for the lower-level skater (prejuvenile to intermediate) to 35 inches for the more mature skater (novice to junior and senior level).

  Medicine Balls. Preferably 6- to 8-inch rubber or leather balls that can be thrown, ranging from 4 to 20 pounds.

  Weighted Jump Ropes. Jump ropes range from 1 to 3 pounds. Jumping rope is a form of plyometrics because the eccentric landing of the jump converts to a concentric jump takeoff. By using a weighted jump rope, the skater must produce greater force to maintain appropriate jump technique or jump rhythm.

  Weight Belts or Weight Vest. These vests or belts are worn around the waist and won't interfere or affect jump technique; they range from .25 pound up to 15 pounds.

6. Plyometric program design and implementation for skaters should be performed by a qualified instructor (see Chapter 3).

7. With plyometric training, the skater must be strong enough to perform the drills with good technique. Good trunk and pelvis control is critical for correct plyometric technique. The following list gives a proper progression of drills, which gradually develops and adapts the muscles and soft tissue.

- Dryland rotational jumps: double-leg and single-leg landing.

- Jumps in place: double leg and single leg.

- Vertical jumps for maximal height.

- Longitudinal jumps for distance: double leg and single leg.

- Box jumps: double leg and single leg.

- Weighted jumps.

- Depth jumps: double-leg and single-leg low-box drop jumps.

Upper/Middle Body Power

- Medicine ball torso rotation drills and passes/tosses.

- Body-weight drills for upper body plyometrics (for example, plyometric push-ups).

PLYOMETRIC BOX
Here is a well-constructed plyometric box: Skaters can get creative and build their own boxes.

MEDICINE BALL
This is a six-pound medicine ball.

WEIGHTED JUMP ROPE
A skater performs a low-intensity plyometric drill with a two-pound weighted jump rope.

SKATER POSITION WITH MEDICINE BALL
The skater is in a start position while holding the medicine ball. Note that the ball is held close to the chest, arms are in, head is up, and torso is straight and tight.

Training Principles

The following principles (techniques) of plyometric training should be emphasized.

1. Appropriate body positioning: head up, shoulders square, torso and back straight, and knees and feet aligned. Skaters should perform jump takeoffs while on the balls of the feet.

2. Explosive takeoff, emphasizing the following:

   • Good knee bend (one-quarter to one-half squat depth) exploding with the hips and legs

   • Quick, explosive double-arm swing with arms

   • Full extension of the ankles, knees, and hips on a majority of the drills

   • Control of jumps or drill movement, including straight body positioning while in the air

3. Control of landing: skater must absorb (eccentrically) the landing with proper alignment of the head, shoulders, torso/back, and knees and feet (knees should be in line with the feet and knees should be placed toward the feet with about a one-quarter knee bend down) and land on the balls of the feet with a slight knee bend.

4. For successful jump/plyometrics, the following should be executed:

   • Maximal effort on all jump/drill attempts

   • Maximal quickness (speed of movement) on rebound jumps off the floor: as soon as the skater makes contact with the floor, he or she must quickly unload and load the neuromuscular structure (ankles, legs, hips, arms) to take off for another jump attempt. The skater must land and take off as quickly as possible, limiting the amount of time on the floor.

5. Torso/abdominal drills are handled in the same manner. This is power training for the core or middle body (abdominal/obliques and lower back muscle groups).

   • Proper body alignment

   • Control of movement

   • Quickness of movement, especially when technique is mastered and when using weighted objects such as medicine balls; for example, when performing medicine ball tosses or passes, catch and throw the ball with a quick arm/shoulder action

   • Maximal effort of the drill

SINGLES: OFF-ICE JUMP/PLYOMETRIC TRAINING AND CORE DRIL

Name: _____   Period: _____   Cycle: _____

Date: _____   Body weight: _____   Body height: _____   Box height: _____

Exercise	Sets	Repetitions	Foot Contacts	Rest Period	Weight
1. Quarter air turns	2	2	32	30 seconds	bwt
Doubles	4	3	12	45 seconds	bwt
Singles	2	3	6	30 seconds	bwt
2. Ankle bounces	3	10	30	1 minute	bwt
3. Quarter squat jumps (double leg)	3	8	24	2 minutes	bwt
4. Lateral box jumps (double leg)	3	8	24	2.5 minutes	bwt
1. Medicine ball torso rotation	4	15		30 seconds	6 pounds
2. Weighted crunches	3	10		30 seconds	2.5 pounds

Total-body flexibility stretching: 15 minutes. Rest periods between jump/plyometric sessions should be at least 48 hours.

Finally, a lot has been discussed about the specific physical benefits obtained from plyometric training, such as increased power and jump height. However, another important, almost hidden, performance characteristic that can be developed from both rotational jump training and plyometric training is kinesthetic awareness, or the skater's ability to recognize his or her body positioning in space. I have seen a tremendous enhancement of body awareness for a number of skaters after six to eight weeks of plyometric jump training. This is especially necessary for preliminary- to intermediate-level skaters who are hard at work developing the necessary motor skills for their technical skill work on-ice (such as

81

double jumps and spins). Specifically, I have noticed that younger skaters while perform-ing jump/plyometric training are initially unable to control and position the head and torso correctly. However, as they put in quality time in off-ice plyometric training, their body/spatial awareness improves, thus allowing them to better position the head, torso, shoulders, and arms when jumping.

QUARTER AIR TURNS (DOUBLE-LEG LANDING)
These are sequential jump air turns in which the skater lands on both feet. The skater begins the air turn in the direction (clockwise or counterclockwise) she rotates on-ice. She performs a quarter turn, then jumps back the opposite way. The skater next performs a half turn and a three-quarter turn, each time jumping back in the oppo-site direction. Finally, she makes a full single turn or rotation, again jumping back in the opposite direction. Make sure the arms pull in and extend on landing, and landings take place on the balls of the feet.

QUARTER AIR TURNS (SINGLE-LEG LANDING)
The skater is performing air turns with a single-leg landing. Concentrate on a quick free-leg and arm extension, while allowing for a good knee bend of the landing leg.

SINGLE JUMP
The skater is attempting a single loop jump.

DOUBLE AXEL JUMP
A skater attempting a double axel on the floor. Note the tight and vertical in-air rotation position.

ANKLE BOUNCES
Dynamic low-intensity plyometric exercise for the ankle/lower legs and arms. Note the skater extending the ankle, and the nice vertical (extended) position in the air. Emphasis should be placed on quick takeoff from the floor, takeoff and landing on the balls of the feet, and finally a jump with maximal height, using a quick double-arm swing.

QUARTER SQUAT JUMPS
The skater performs the quarter squat jump from the start position with a knee bend to takeoff and full extension of the ankle, knee, and hips, and finally landing. Note that the skater has a good posture: head is up, shoulders are square, and feet are shoulder-width apart. The skater is taking off and landing on the balls of the feet with appropriate knee bend to absorb the jump landing. Key points are not letting the knees go past the toes on take-off and landing and using an explosive double-arm swing to generate more power at takeoff. Landing and takeoff should be as quick as possible, minimizing the amount of time on the ground.

DOUBLE-LEG LATERAL BOX JUMPS
This skater is performing the plyometric lateral box jump. In the start position, the skater stands erect on the box with a slight knee bend. The skater then drops or steps off the box, landing on the balls of the feet, and then quickly accelerates into a takeoff jump back onto the box. The skater lands on the box with arms checked out. Landing should be soft, on the balls of the feet, with torso straight and erect and knees slightly bent. Box jumps should have a quick, explosive takeoff from the floor and land on the middle of the box, with a quick check-out of the arms. Finally, when landing on the floor, the skater needs to decelerate, absorbing the jump with the knee bend, and with ankle, knee, and hip extension the skater then quickly accelerates into takeoff.

MEDICINE BALL TORSO ROTATION

Here the skater is performing a speed/strength rotation movement of the torso. In the start position, the medicine ball is held close to the chest area, feet are stable on the floor with the legs crossed to simulate an in-air rotation position, and the arms are held in. The skater rotates the torso (second photo), keeping the shoulders square; head remains still, and the hips remain stable. Rotation should be a full–range of motion twisting from side to side.

WEIGHTED CRUNCHES

The skater is performing resistance crunches. In the start position, the skater is flat on the mat, feet are flat against the wall, and the knee and hip are at a ninety-degree angle. The medicine ball is held high on the chest with both hands. The skater contracts the abdominals to lift the shoulder blades off the floor, and then returns to the start position. The key is to keep the head stable and lift and lower the upper torso with a slow, controlled movement.

PAIRS: OFF-ICE JUMP/PLYOMETRIC TRAINING AND CORE DRILL SHEET

Name: _____ Period: _____ Cycle: _____

Date: _____ Body weight: _____ Body height: _____ Box height: _____

Exercise	Sets	Repetitions	Foot Contacts	Rest Period	Weight
1. Quarter air turns	2	2	32	30 seconds	bwt
Doubles[a]	4	3	12	45 seconds	bwt
Singles[b]	2	3	6	30 seconds	bwt
2. Ankle bounces[c]	3	10	30	1 minute	bwt
3. Quarter squat jumps (double leg)[d]	3	8	24	2 minutes	bwt
4. Medicine ball chest pass	3	8	24	2 minutes	6 pounds

Exercise	Sets	Repetitions	Foot Contacts	Rest Period	Weight
1. Medicine ball lateral toss	4	15		2 minutes	6 pounds
2. Weighted crunches[e]	3	10		30 seconds	2.5 pounds

Total-body flexibility stretching: 15 minutes. Rest periods between jump/plyometric sessions should be at least 48 hours.

a. See page 82.
b. See page 82.
c. See page 83.
d. See page 84.
e. See page 85.

MEDICINE BALL CHEST PASS

This partner medicine ball chest pass is an excellent upper and middle body plyometric drill. Skaters are approximately six to eight apart, facing each other. The drill begins with a chest pass of the medicine ball from one skater to the other. The medicine ball should be thrown from the chest area, extending the arms straight out. Feet remain flat on the ground; all movement is from the chest, shoulders, and arms. The ball is caught with arms extended. The arms are drawn into the chest and then quickly extended out to throw to the partner. The ball should be caught and thrown with as much force as possible and as quickly as possible.

MEDICINE BALL LATERAL TOSS

These photos depict another torso rotation drill using the medicine ball. Skaters are positioned laterally, six to eight feet apart. The skater must rotate or twist to the side and generate momentum to throw the medicine ball to the opposite side to the partner. Notice the bend in the elbows. Hips should be stabilized or still; all the movement should be with the torso and arms. For this drill to be executed appropriately, the ball should be caught to one side, and then the skater rotates to the opposite side and back to throw to the partner as quickly as possible and with as much force as possible in the throw.

ICE DANCE: OFF-ICE JUMP/PLYOMETRIC TRAINING AND CORE DRILL SHEET

Name: _____   Period: _____   Cycle: _____

Date: _____   Body weight: _____   Body height: _____   Box height: _____

Exercise	Sets	Repetitions	Foot Contacts	Rest Period	Weight
1. Ankle bounces[a]	3	10	30	1 minute	bwt
2. Zigzag jumps (double leg)	3	8	24	2 minutes	bwt
3. Medicine ball chest pass[b]	3	8	24	2 minutes	6 pounds
1. Weighted crunches[c]	3	10		30 seconds	2.5 pounds
2. Medicine ball lateral toss[d]	3	8		2 minutes	6 pounds

Total-body flexibility stretching: 15 minutes. Rest periods between jump/plyometric sessions should be at least 48 hours.

a. See page 83.
b. See page 87.
c. See page 85.
d. See page 87.

ZIGZAG JUMPS DOUBLE LEG
In the start position, the skater has feet shoulder-width apart, arms in the power position, knees bent, and torso erect. The movement begins with a diagonal jump out, landing on the balls of the feet, and then quickly accelerating to jump in the opposite diagonal direction, making a zigzag formation across the floor. Notice that the ice dancer is extending with the ankles, knees, and hips; however, the key for good technique is for the ice dancer to stay close to the floor and perform a jump with more horizontal distance instead of vertical height (singles and pairs skater are more concerned about jumping for height as opposed to the ice dancer, who needs more horizontal distance during plyometric drills).

PLYOMETRIC TRAINING LOG

Name: _____   Program: _____   Rest Periods: _____   Warm-Up: _____   Phase: _____

Start Date: _____

Singles

bwt = body weight as resistance

Exercise	sets		1/1	1/2	1/3	1/4										
Quarter Air Turns		lbs.	bwt	bwt												
		reps.	2	2												
Singles		lbs.	bwt	bwt												
		reps.	3	3												
Doubles		lbs.	bwt	bwt	bwt	bwt										
		reps.	3	3	3	3										
Ankle Bounces		lbs.	bwt	bwt	bwt											
		reps.	10	10	10											
Double-Leg Quarter Squat Jumps		lbs.	bwt	bwt	bwt											
		reps.	8	8	8											
Double-Leg Lateral Box Jumps (Box Ht= ")		lbs.	bwt	bwt	bwt											
		reps.	8	8	8											
Medicine Ball Torso Rotation		lbs.	6	6	6	6										
		reps.	15	15	15	15										
Weighted Crunches		lbs.	2.5	2.5	2.5											
		reps.	10	10	10											
Stretching: Total Body	duration															
How do you feel?																
Intensity of Workout																

PLYOMETRIC TRAINING LOG

Name: _____ Program: _____ Rest Periods: _____ Warm-Up: _____ Phase: _____

Start Date: _____

Pairs

bwt = body weight as resistance

Exercise	sets	1/1	1/2	1/3	1/4																			
Quarter Air Turns	lbs.	bwt	bwt																					
	reps.	2	2																					
Singles	lbs.	bwt	bwt																					
	reps.	3	3																					
Doubles	lbs.	bwt	bwt	bwt																				
	reps.	3	3	3	3																			
Ankle Bounces	lbs.	bwt	bwt	bwt																				
	reps.	10	10	10																				
Double-Leg Quarter Squat Jumps	lbs.	bwt	bwt	bwt																				
	reps.	8	8	8																				
Medicine Ball Chest Pass	lbs.	6	6	6																				
	reps.	8	8	8																				
Medicine Ball Lateral Toss	lbs.	6	6	6	6																			
	reps.	15	15	15	15																			
Weighted Crunches	lbs.	2.5	2.5	2.5																				
	reps.	10	10	10																				
Stretching: Total Body	duration																							
How do you feel?																								
Intensity of Workout																								

PLYOMETRIC TRAINING LOG

Name: _____ Program: _____ Rest Periods: _____ Warm-Up: _____ Phase: _____

Start Date: _____ **Ice Dance**

bwt = body weight as resistance

Exercise	sets	1/1	1/2	1/3	1/4											
Ankle Bounces	lbs.	bwt	bwt	bwt												
	reps.	10	10	10												
Double-Leg Zig Zag Jumps	lbs.	bwt	bwt	bwt												
	reps.	8	8	8												
Medicine Ball Chest Pass	lbs.	6	6	6												
	reps.	8	8	8												
Medicine Ball Lateral Toss	lbs.	6	6	6												
	reps.	8	8	8												
Weighted Crunches	lbs.	2.5	2.5	2.5												
	reps.	10	10	10												
	lbs.															
	reps.															
	lbs.															
	reps.															
	lbs.															
	reps.															
Stretching: Total Body	duration															
How do you feel?																
Intensity of Workout																

CHAPTER 6

Endurance Conditioning
for Skating

Probably the most researched physical performance component of skating is cardiovascular conditioning. Everyone agrees that in order for a skater to complete a technically difficult program lasting four minutes or longer with well-versed choreography, a high level of both aerobic and anaerobic cardiovascular fitness or conditioning must be present. Aerobic and anaerobic conditioning energy systems can be defined as follows:

Aerobic. This system requires oxygen for long-term physical activity. It relies on a skater's cardiovascular capacity (ability to efficiently breathe air) to produce energy for movement.

Anaerobic. This system functions without oxygen and causes the accumulation of waste products in the muscles and blood, such as lactic acid. The anaerobic energy system can be further classified into the immediate or ATP–CP system and the short-term or glycolysis (lactic acid) system. In the anaerobic energy system, the skater uses energy already stored in the body to produce movement.

Table 6.1 lists all the energy systems and their respective abilities to supply energy for activities at various intensities and durations. During physical activity, all three energy systems (oxidative/aerobic, anaerobic/immediate, and anaerobic glycolysis) are active at specific times. Important to skating a short or long program, however, is that the extent to which each system is utilized depends mainly on the intensity of that program.

TABLE 6.1   ENERGY SYSTEM COMPONENTS

Energy System	Power	Capacity	Duration of Activity
ATP–CP (anaerobic or immediate)	High	Low	Up to 30 seconds
Lactic acid (anaerobic or short term)	Moderate	Moderate/High	30–180 seconds
Oxidative (aerobic or long term)	Low	High	Greater than 180 seconds or 3 minutes

As discussed in Chapter 1, the intensity or skill level of a skater's program will determine the extent of energy production. Secondarily, duration of activity determines which energy system is used. Since all skating programs are relatively short (short programs last approximately two minutes, long programs four minutes), energy is produced primarily through anaerobic (glycolysis) activity. Figure-skating programs cause anaerobic stress; within this two- to three-minute duration, skaters perform a log of highly technical, demanding movements (jumps, spins, footwork, pairs lifts, and dance lifts) that are characteristic of ATP–CP or immediate anaerobic energy production. Even fast-velocity stroking can yield high levels of anaerobic activity. Figure 6.1 represents actual energy system capacities related to figure-skating skill components. The figure portrays a scale of all three energy systems and their work capacities. Note the skills listed under their respective durations. From this, skaters can see that the more technical skills require more energy in a short time period. See Table 1.4, page 9.

Endurance-conditioning properties for figure skating incorporate physiological training of both the cardiovascular and pulmonary systems (heart, lungs). From a physiological standpoint, what occurs as a skater competes in a long program? Even before the start of a program, skaters may experience elevated heart and respiratory rates due to anxiety levels and from their warm-ups. As skaters begin their programs, their heart rates reach maximal levels after about a minute and stay elevated for the duration of the program. Corresponding to elevated heart and respiratory rates is the accumulation of lactic acid within the blood and muscles. As skaters reach a maximal or even supramaximal effort, lactic acid accumulates markedly, interfering with performance. Skaters that feel a tight, burning sensation in their legs or arms halfway through their long programs know the effects of lactic acid. Fatigue waste products may impair jumps, especially of the takeoff leg, pairs and dance lifts, and overall choreography movements, especially with the arms. Fatigue can also impair judgment and concentration during a program, resulting in errors or missed elements.

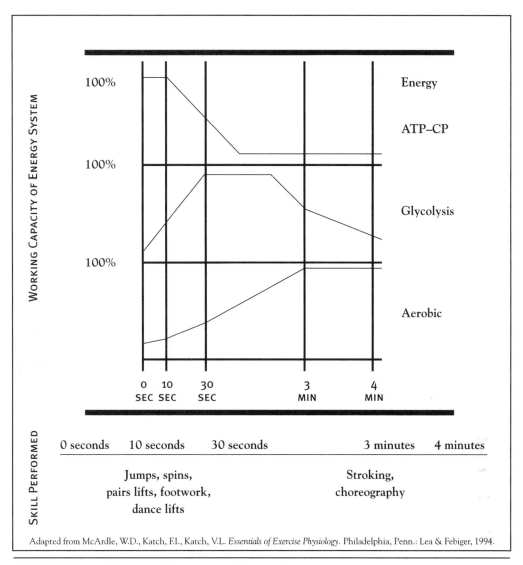

FIGURE 6.1   WORKING CAPACITY OF ENERGY SYSTEMS

I have seen over and over the inability of skaters to complete or finish their long programs with the needed power, endurance, strength, and quality of presentation. It is one thing to practice the skill work of jumps, spins, stroking, and choreography separately; it is another thing to put the pieces together into an entire program executed without mistakes and with a full degree of available energy.

I have tested on-ice program heart rates for all levels, juvenile to senior. This direct measurement of intensity shows a maximal and even supramaximal capacity when the skater performs the free-skate or long program (heart rates as high as 210 beats per minute). So how should skaters train or condition themselves?

A skater on-ice checks her heart rate reading.

To begin with, conditioning for figure skating must be individualized, practical, and structured in a level-specific way. For example, a juvenile- or intermediate-level skater will not have the same endurance conditioning needs as a junior- or senior-level skater. Efficiency is the key factor that enables a skater to benefit from a conditioning program. No matter what skaters do off-ice or on-ice for their endurance conditioning, if it is not structured toward practical, specific efficiency work, the results may not benefit the skater. For example, only jogging off-ice for endurance conditioning is not closely related enough to a skater's on-ice program to be effective. Higher-intensity skill exercises must be combined with stressful aerobic and anaerobic drills. Skaters must condition themselves specific to their actual performance. Improperly designed endurance-training programs that are not specific to figure skating may actually be detrimental to a skater's speed, power, and skill. An appropriate endurance-conditioning program for figure skating must consider the following:

1. Training both aerobic and anaerobic energy systems.
2. Meeting the specific demands of the sport: its high intensity (high heart rate and lactic acid accumulation) and highly skilled movements.
3. Individualizing the program relative to the skater's age, level, and, possibly, body weight.
4. Periodizing the program so that the skater does not overtrain with endurance conditioning, which can be detrimental to performance.

In summary, the following physical characteristics take place in a four-minute long program:

1. Skaters normally begin their programs with a somewhat elevated heart rate due to anxiety and other related stressors. I have tested start heart rates ranging from 108 to 150 beats per minute (bpm).
2. During the first minute of the long program, the intensity reaches maximal levels due to the technical aspect of the program (stroking into the first jump combination or jumps, pairs/dance lifts, and other related movements).

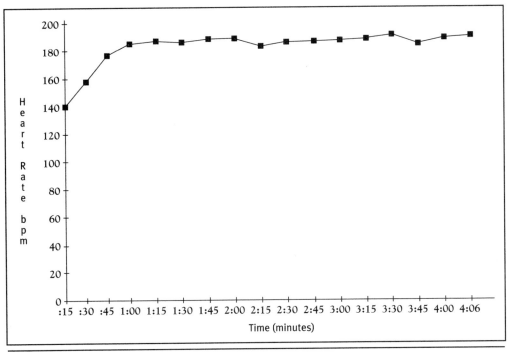

FIGURE 6.2   LONG PROGRAM HEART RATE DATA AND GRAPH CURVE:
AUGUST 24, 1994

3. Intensity levels (heart rate and lactate accumulation) are maintained throughout the duration of the long program, only reducing somewhat during the slow section of a skater's program.

Figure 6.2 is a sample heart rate plot of a nineteen-year-old female senior skater preparing for sectionals qualifying competition. Note the accelerated increase in heart rate and program intensity with a maximal heart rate of 193 bpm, which was maintained for the duration of the program. After eleven weeks of endurance training, the skater's start heart rate dropped off from 139 on August 24 to 116 on November 10 (see Figures 6.2 and 6.3). Also, note the differences in total heart rates at each fifteen-second interval. Overall, this skater benefited from her conditioning training, exemplifying a more efficient long program run-through, based on her heart rate readings. Also, this skater performed her jumps and elements more effectively during the posttest program on November 10, landing more total triple jumps and jump combinations.

Skaters who perform more efficiently early in their long programs will have more energy available for the latter part of the program. A skater who starts his or her program with a lower heart rate may experience less stress, thus avoiding the errors that can result from high stress.

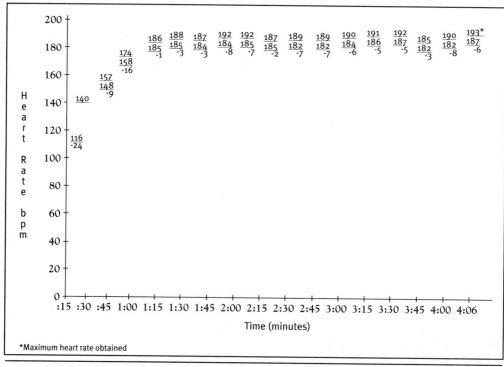

FIGURE 6.3 Long Program Heart Rate Pretest and Posttest Data and Graph Curve: November 10, 1994

So how do we put all this conditioning information into a program design for the figure skater? Chapter 8 describes in detail a yearly conditioning plan. When I design conditioning programs for figure skaters, I take into account the following:

1. Age and competitive level of the skater
2. Jump or skill technique level of the skater
3. Body fat (the skater may need to lose some body fat, keeping in mind that body fat levels are naturally higher in female skaters)
4. Periodization factors, such as the skater's need to peak for a specific time or competition, whether the skater is involved in on-ice stroking or power sessions, and how many freestyles, pairs, or ice dance sessions the skater is performing per day or week

The following step-by-step endurance-conditioning cycle may be used for supplemental endurance training.

Step-by-Step Endurance-Conditioning Cycle

1. Test skaters while they perform their long programs (full run-through) in the off-season or as soon as the program is set with all planned elements (jumps, spins, footwork, and choreography). If available, skaters may be tested specifically for maximal oxygen uptake (VO2 max), pulmonary function, and maximal and average heart rate variables. These tests must be scheduled through a local sports medicine or sports physiology lab.

2. Set up appropriate aerobic and anaerobic training zones; use test heart rate maximums or age-predicted maximums.

   Aerobic: 70 to 85 percent of maximal program heart rate

   Anaerobic: 85 to 95 percent of maximal program heart rate

   Example: Maximal program heart rate = 193 bpm

   Aerobic target heart rate (THR) =   193 × .70 = 135 bpm

                                            193 × .85 = 164 bpm

   Aerobic THR zone =   135–164 bpm

   Anaerobic THR =   193 × .85 = 164 bpm

                                            193 × .95 = 183 bpm

   Anaerobic THR zone =   164–183 bpm

   Use this formula for age-predicted heart rate zones when the skater cannot test for maximal heart rate: 220 – age (years) = maximal heart rate.

   Example: 220 – 16 years =   204

                204 × .70 percent =   143

                204 × .85 percent =   173

                294 × .95 percent =   194

   Aerobic age-related maximal THR zone =   143 – 173 bpm

   Anaerobic age-related maximal THR zone = 173 – 194 bpm

   (continued overleaf)

See Table 6.2 for age-related target heart rate intensities. If the skater's long program maximal heart rate is lower than his or her age-predicted heart rate, that value (age-predicted maximal heart rate) should be used in determining the aerobic and anaerobic training zones. This would enable the skater to begin training at a higher heart rate zone (higher intensity from the start of the endurance conditioning).

TABLE 6.2   AGE-RELATED HEART RATE INTENSITY ZONES: 10 TO 30 YEARS OF AGE
(BOTH AEROBIC AND ANAEROBIC TRAINING ZONES)

Age	Maximal Heart Rate	Intensity Percentages		
		70%	85%	95%
10	210	147	178	199
11	209	146	177	198
12	208	145	176	197
13	207	144	175	196
14	206	144	175	195
15	205	143	174	194
16	204	142	173	193
17	203	142	172	192
18	202	141	171	192
19	201	140	170	191
20	200	140	170	190
21	199	139	169	189
22	198	138	168	188
23	197	138	168	187
24	196	137	166	186
25	195	136	166	185
26	194	136	166	184
27	193	135	164	183
28	192	134	163	182
29	191	133	162	181
30	190	133	161	180

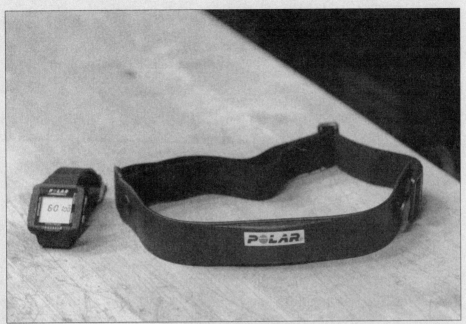

The heart rate monitor consists of the transmitter and strap, which goes around the skater's chest, and the watch, which is worn around the wrist. Skaters can see their heart rate readings while they are conditioning or performing.

3. Skaters should learn how to measure their heart rate (pulse): Find the pulse by pressing the fingertips of the forefinger and middle finger on the radial artery (wrist area on the thumb side); count heartbeats for 10 seconds and multiply by 6. For example, 30 beats in a 10-second count: 30 × 6 = 180 bpm. Heart rate monitors may also be used for both on-ice and off-ice endurance conditioning and evaluation. Heart rate monitors are a valuable tool to monitor or determine appropriate heart rate zones or training intensities. This piece of equipment simplifies reading heart rates; it allows the skater to know his or her heart rate while exercising without having to stop exercise to manually check the pulse.

4. Design the skater's base aerobic program (see drills record sheet on page 103). Note that the choices of exercises range from most specific to exercises with less stress to the joint areas (hip, lower back, knee, ankle). This program should be implemented in the early off-season.

    Skaters can use the drills record sheet to perform each endurance-conditioning component (aerobic, anaerobic basic, or anaerobic tactical); the sheet lists the exercises in a specific order and details volume, intensities, and rest periods. The skater can use the drill record sheet to go through endurance-training sessions and to track his or her exercise-training

(continued overleaf)

variables. Another important aspect of the drills record sheet is that it gives the skater a choice in what conditioning exercises he or she can perform. No matter what exercise equipment the skater has access to, he or she can use the drill sheet for information on volume, intensity, and rest period.

5. Design the skater's anaerobic training program (see drills record sheet on page 105). Note that this program should be implemented in the late pre-season and in-season.

6. Design and implement tactical, high-intensity interval training. This should be specific to the structure of the long or freestyle program. Skaters should try to complete conditioning on the ice when possible; however, they can utilize the tactical off-ice circuit program if they need to perform their conditioning off-ice (see drills record sheets on pages 106, 110, and 115).

ON-ICE STROKING
An intermediate-level skater is stroking on-ice with the help of the heart rate monitor: note the heart rate monitor watch that is worn on her left wrist. The technical coach can assist in designing the actual stroking patterns, which would include continuous stroking using forward and backward crossovers, utilizing the whole ice surface, with the addition of various field moves patterns. The goal is to perform steady-state stroking that is continuous for the entire twenty- to thirty-minute duration.

DRILLS RECORD SHEET

Name: _____   Phase: _____   Time period: _____   Date: _____

Frequency: 2–3 times per week   Target heart rate training zone: _____   Body weight: _____

Drill Name	Mode, Elements	Set #	Duration	Heart Rate	Recovery Time
1. Aerobic	On-ice stroking		20–30 minutes	70–85 %	0
2.	Slideboard		20–30 minutes	70–85 %	0
3.	Treadmill		20–30 minutes	70–85 %	0
4.	Cross-trainer		20–30 minutes	70–85 %	0
5.	Stair-stepper		20–30 minutes	70–85 %	0
6.	Cycle		20–30 minutes	70–85 %	

Totals: _____

Note: Must remain in target heart rate zone. Cool down 5 minutes with total-body flexibility stretching for 15 m

SLIDEBOARD CONDITIONING
Here the skater is using the slideboard as a mode of conditioning. This skater is also checking his exercise intensity by monitoring his heart rate on his watch.

TREADMILL CONDITIONING
The same skater is shown training on the treadmill. The treadmill provides excellent aerobic and anaerobic training. The majority of skaters have an excellent heart rate response while using the treadmill. A majority of treadmills now have a "soft" landing surface, reducing landing impact forces.

BACK SQUAT TACTICAL CIRCUIT TRAINING
Here the same back squat techniques as described in Chapter 3 are implemented in the tactical circuit program. Since back squats are a total-body, multijoint strength exercise, by performing this exercise, the athlete will experience a large metabolic or energy output. Thus, this particular exercise can have a positive or high heart rate response and postexercise metabolic increase even though it is typically used for strength/power.

DRILLS RECORD SHEET

Name: _____   Phase: _____   Time period: _____   Date: _____

Frequency: 2–3 times per week   Target heart rate training zone: _____   Body weight: _____

Drill Name	Mode, Elements	Set #	Duration	Heart Rate	Recovery Time
1. Anaerobic intervals	On-ice stroking intervals or kill drill	4–8	1–4 minutes	85–95 %	30 seconds–2 minutes
2.	Slideboard	4–8	1–4 minutes	85–95%	30 seconds–2 minutes
3.	Treadmill	4–8	1–4 minutes	85–95%	30 seconds–2 minutes
4.	Cross-trainer	4–8	1–4 minutes	85–95%	30 seconds–2 minutes
5.	Stair-stepper	4–8	1–4 minutes	85–95%	30 seconds–1 minute
6.	Cycle	4–8	1–4 minutes	85–95%	30 seconds–2 minutes

Totals: _____

Note: Must remain in target heart rate zone. Cool down 5 minutes with total-body flexibility stretching for 15 minutes.

DRILLS RECORD SHEET (Singles)

Name: _____   Phase: _____   Time period: _____   Date: _____

Frequency: 1–2 times per week   Target heart rate training zone: _____   Body weight: _____

Drill Name	Mode, Elements	Set/Reps Wts.	Duration	Heart Rate	Recovery Time
1. Tactical Circuit	Back squats[a]	____ lb.	1 minute	85–95%	30 seconds
2.	Split-leg cycle jumps	n = 30		85–95%	30 seconds
3.	Slideboard		2 minutes	85–95%	30 seconds
4.	Jump rotations doubles	2 × 2			30 seconds
5.	Weighted jump rope	____ lb.	1 minute	85–95%	30 seconds
6.	Medicine ball torso wall throws	____ lb.	30 seconds		30 seconds
7.	Cariocas footwork		2 minutes	85–95%	30 seconds
8.	Jump rotations doubles	2 × 2			

Totals: _____

Repeats: n = _____

Note: Start circuit with heart rate at least 120 beats per minute or higher. Skater must rest at least 3–5 minutes before starting another cir-

SPLIT-LEG CYCLE JUMPS

The skater is performing a dynamic low- to moderate-intensity plyometric jump drill. Note the start position of the skater with legs split from front to back. The skater begins the takeoff with ankle, knee, and hip flexion, then extension at takeoff: the skater bends at the knee and hips, and then takes off into the air. In the final position in the air, the skater has split and exchanged leg positions. The skater begins the jump with the right leg behind, then while in the air, kicks the right leg through. Note the excellent extension of the legs, and how the skater used her arms to drive the body off the floor and into the air. Landing should be on the balls of the feet, with the legs still in the split position. Only in the air do the legs travel side by side to continue into a split position. Split-leg cycle jumps will produce a high-energy output due to the dynamic or total-body, explosive nature of performing the exercise. This drill is good for the heart rate response and to simulate "kicking-through" for axel jump. The athlete can perform this technical drill for technique while fatigued.

SLIDEBOARD CONDITIONING

The skater is using the slideboard as part of the circuit program. The technique should involve adequate knee bend for the leg push, shoulders square, head stable; the torso should be upright and erect. Note the use of the arms by the skater to provide extra power in the stroke.

DOUBLE OR TRIPLE JUMP ROTATIONS

These two photos show the next tactical circuit station, dryland jump rotations. Here the skater performed a double loop on the floor. Floor rotations are used in the tactical circuit to provide a specific drill: training the jump rotation in a fatigued state. This increases or at least maintains exercise heart rate, from a technical skating-specific power drill, providing a stimulus for anaerobic/tactical conditioning.

WEIGHTED JUMP ROPE
This skater is demonstrating good technique with the weighted jump rope. Note the skater jumping on the balls of the feet, with good posture and control. By using a heavier jump rope (one to three pounds), skaters can have an adequate heart rate response and respiratory rate. The weighted jump rope also necessitates more force production from the shoulders and upper back muscles, which would be good for pairs and ice dance skaters.

MEDICINE BALL WALL THROWS
The skater is performing a dynamic torso drill called medicine ball wall throw, throwing a medicine ball into the wall for a designated time. Note the body positioning of the skater: feet are shoulder-width apart, the medicine ball is held close to the chest area, arms are in. The movement begins with a rotation to the side of the body opposite the wall; then as the skater rotates the torso toward the wall, the ball is released and thrown into the wall. The skater then catches the ball rebounding off the wall and rotates back to the start position. It is recommended that skaters perform this drill rotating in both directions: left side of body toward the wall, then right side of body toward the wall. Emphasis should be placed on body positioning, power of the throw, and quickness of the torso rotation. Feet must remain firm against the floor. Although not recognized as an endurance-conditioning drill, the medicine ball wall throw can maintain the heart rate due to the dynamics of this particular exercise. Technique for this drill requires a large production of power or force of the arms, shoulders, upper back, and torso. The main emphasis for this exercise, especially since it is near the end of the tactical circuit program, is to provide some form of strength-endurance training for the torso area.

CARIOCAS, FOOTWORK DRILL

This circuit station is another conditioning station that trains the quickness of the feet and hip/torso areas. This total-body endurance or speed-endurance drill will elevate the heart rate dramatically, thus producing a good conditioning effect. Note that the skater is always on the balls of the feet, arms are held up and out, and the torso stabilized. The movement patterns are a continuous crossover step of the legs across the floor, with each leg alternating in front to back. Emphasis should be on body control, footwork speed, and torso stability.

JUMP ROTATIONS

The final station is a repeat of the double and/or triple jump rotations. At this point in the circuit program, each skater needs to concentrate on good technique (correct body position, tight in-air rotation position, quick check-out with good free-leg and arm extension and good knee bend on the landing leg), which is especially hard because fatigue can hinder jump performance.

DRILLS RECORD SHEET (Pairs)

Name: _____ Phase: _____ Time period: _____ Date: _____

Frequency: 1–2 times per week   Target heart rate training zone: _____   Body weight: _____

Drill Name	Mode, Elements	Set/Reps Wts.	Duration	Heart Rate	Recovery Time
1. Tactical Circuit	Back squats	____ lb.	1 minute	85–95%	30 seconds
2.	Tuck jumps	n = 30			
3.	Slideboard		2 minutes		
4.	Push press	____ lb.	8–12 reps		
5.	Jump rotations doubles*	2 × 2			
6.	Weighted jump rope	____ lb.	2 minutes		
7.	Medicine ball sit-up with pass	____ lb.	1 minute		
8.	Cariocas footwork		45 seconds		

Totals: _____

Repeats: n = _____   *May substitute dryland pairs lifts.

Note: Start circuit with heart rate at least 120 beats per minute or higher. Skater must rest at least 3–5 minutes before starting another circuit. *Must remain in target heart rate zone.* Cool down 5 minutes with total-body flexibility stretching for 15 minutes.

BACK SQUATS
These photos show the same technique used for the singles circuit program for the start of the pairs tactical circuit run-through.

| Start position. | Middle position 1. | Middle position 2. | Finish position. |

TUCK JUMPS
These photos show sequences of the hip/knee dynamic plyometric jump drill tuck jumps. In the start or standard power position, the skater flexes the knees and hips, then slightly extends the ankles, knees, and hips, jumping into the air. In the midair position, the knees are near the chest. This exaggerated movement (flexed knee position) increases the vertical height of the jump. The skater must concentrate on keeping the shoulders square and the back as straight as possible, with the torso erect. A double-arm swing increases the power of this exercise. The skater should land on the balls of the feet, quickly unloading the landing and loading the leg and hip muscles to accelerate into another takeoff. Tuck jumps are similar to split-leg cycle jumps in that they will also produce an elevated heart rate response even though the exercise lasts only a short time.

SLIDEBOARD
Pairs skaters can also use the slideboard as a mode of conditioning to elevate the heart rate and respiratory rate, as part of the circuit program.

PUSH PRESS
This total-body strength/power lift can be used by the pairs skater, especially as an upper body strength component in the circuit program (see Chapter 3, pairs strength exercises). Similar to back squats, the push press is obviously a total-body, multiple-joint lift that has an excellent metabolic carryover.

JUMP ROTATIONS
Floor double- and triple-jump rotations are the next station for the pairs circuit program. At this point in the circuit, fatigue may be a factor, so skaters must concentrate even more on appropriate jump technique.

WEIGHTED JUMP ROPE
This is the same drill as used in the singles circuit. Pairs skaters may use a heavier jump rope since their overall upper body strength and power is typically greater than the singles skater.

MEDICINE BALL SIT-UP WITH PASS
These pairs skaters are performing a dynamic weighted abdominal exercise. In the start position the body is in the standard sit-up position with knees bent and feet flat. One skater holds a medicine ball close to his chest; the feet of both skaters are close together (skaters can interlock feet if needed). The skater flexes the abdominals, lifting his upper body off the floor toward the top of his knees. As he comes up at the top of the movement, he tosses the ball to his partner. The other skater catches the ball with arms slightly extended, and then under control, lowers her torso/upper body down to the floor to the start position. The key is to use the abdominals and limit use of the hips by elevating the body in a controlled manner, keeping the back as straight as possible, shoulders square, and head stable. To make this drill more technical, the medicine ball can be held overhead throughout the full range of motion. This drill, like the medicine ball wall throw, is put near the end of the pairs tactical circuit program to train the middle body for strength and endurance.

113

CARIOCAS
This skater is performing the same footwork drill as the singles skater. Again, this is an excellent drill for footwork quickness and hip/torso control. Also, with pairs skaters the upper body should be strong through this drill, especially as it is at the end of their circuit program.

DRILLS RECORD SHEET (Ice Dance)

Name: _____   Phase: _____   Time period: _____   Date: _____

Frequency: 1–2 times per week   Target heart rate training zone: _____   Body weight: _____

Drill Name	Mode, Elements	Set/Reps Wts.	Duration	Heart Rate	Recovery Time
1. Tactical Circuit	Walking front lunges	____ lb.	1 minute	85–95%	30 seconds
2.	Single-leg lateral strides	n = 20			
3.	Slideboard		2 minutes		
4.	Push press	____ lb.	8–12 reps		
5.	Weighted jump rope	____ lb.	2 minutes		
6.	Cycle crunches*		45 seconds		
7.	Cariocas footwork		2 minutes		
8.	Standing medicine ball lateral toss	____ lb.	45 seconds		

Totals: _____

Repeats: n = _____   *May substitute dryland dance lifts.

Note: Start circuit with heart rate at least 120 beats per minute or higher. Skater must rest at least 3–5 minutes before starting another circuit. *Must remain in target heart rate zone.* Cool down 5 minutes with total-body flexibility stretching for 15 minutes.

WALKING FRONT LUNGES

This continuous lower body (and some middle body) strength exercise is great for ice dancers. In photo 1, the same start position is used as with the regular lunge. Note the body positioning of the skater and the bar placement, resting just above the shoulder blades and supported by the hands. The skater lifts the stride leg and steps out moving forward (2nd photo). Note the good vertical posture; the knee is over the middle of the lead foot, with eventual knee bend until the top of the thigh is parallel to the floor. The back leg has a slight knee bend; however, the knee should not touch the floor. Once the initial stride is taken, the skater then quickly, with control, steps into another stride with the opposite leg (3rd photo). The key is to stride with a straight, not rounded, back. The knee should be aligned with the foot; however, the knee needs to stay over the middle of the foot. The stride foot must remain flat on the floor, shoulders square and head straight. This exercise can have a positive endurance or metabolic strength-conditioning effect due to the continuous multi-joint strength movement. The working muscles are total body; therefore, the energy output is high. Again, this exercise is a continuous movement across the floor.

SINGLE-LEG LATERAL STRIDES

This ice dancer is performing a dynamic stride/jump; he jumps or pushes off one leg laterally (start position), landing on the ball of the foot on the opposite leg (finish position), and then quickly shifts his weight and jumps off the landing foot back to the start side. Landing and takeoff must be as quick as possible. It is very important to use the arms for body control and to maintain good middle body posture. This is an excellent drill for body control and awareness and will produce a high heart rate postexercise, thus allowing the skater to complete the exercise and continue to the slideboard despite fatigue.

SLIDEBOARD

The same slideboard mode is used for conditioning effect; however, ice dancers can get creative by sliding in various movement patterns.

PUSH PRESS
This is the same strength/power exercise for total body as performed by the pairs skater.

WEIGHTED JUMP ROPE
This is a total-body dynamic exercise to elevate the heart rate and breathing rate. Again, ice dancers, same as the pairs skaters, may want to use a heavier jump rope (three to four pounds).

CYCLE CRUNCHES
This is a dynamic core body drill/exercise (for technique detail, see ice dance strength exercises in Chapter 3). Cycle crunches are used for strength-endurance training of the torso area.

CARIOCAS
This footwork drill is the same as for singles and pairs skaters; however, ice dancers may want to perform more hip movements with this drill, with more of a twisting movement of the hips and torso area.

Start position.

Middle position 1.

Middle position 2.

Middle position 3.

Middle position 4.

Middle position 5.

Middle position 6.

Final position.

STANDING MEDICINE BALL LATERAL TOSS

These photos show a torso power exercise, using partners with the medicine ball. In the start position, the skaters are positioned side by side; one skater holds a medicine ball, arms slightly extended. The skater with the ball rotates or twists to the opposite side (middle position 1), and then rotates back around; the ball is tossed or thrown to his partner (middle position 2). The partner catches the ball off his shoulder side (middle positions 3 and 4), rotates around to the opposite side (middle position 5), and then back (middle position 6), tossing the ball back to the start partner (final position). The key is to always keep the feet firm on the ground and the hips stable. This drill isolates the torso area, using only the muscle movements of the torso, not the hips. Finally, the medicine ball should always be aligned in the middle body and thrown with the shoulders square. Do not throw with the arms moving the ball to the side or outside of the middle body or chest area. Once good technique is established, skaters should perform this drill as quickly as possible.

SPECIFICITY: ON-ICE ENDURANCE CONDITIONING

Conditioning on-ice may be used, incorporating variations of the previously mentioned energy systems:

- On-ice continuous stroking (aerobic conditioning)

- On-ice interval stroking (aerobic and anaerobic glycolysis conditioning)

- On-ice simulated program work and kill drills (anaerobic lactate, ATP–CP training, and aerobic)

The following sample drill record sheets on pages 122–128 are basic on-ice conditioning programs. The skater can use these drills to build skating-specific endurance conditioning. Keep in mind that these are basic, one-variation drills. The skater and coach can further vary the elements, duration, rest periods, frequency, and intensity (microcycle or weekly periodization). Individualize these drills specific to the ability of the skater.

THE DRILLS DATA SHEET

The drills sheet on page 122 is a basic data sheet for the skater to track the drill mode, heart rate data, duration, training zone, and rest periods. This drill sheet is handy for the skater to use each session he or she attempts conditioning to monitor the various training variables. This data sheet should be used in conjunction with the drills record sheets, which track individual drill elements.

INTERVAL STROKING DRILL
A skater is stroking at a high-intensity level (anaerobic).

INTERVAL STROKING DRILL WITH JUMP ATTEMPT
The same skater is attempting a triple axel within the same interval stroking drill.

ON-ICE HEART RATE READING
A heart rate response of a skater who is taking a rest from an interval stroking drill. Note that the high heart rate (182 beats per minute) reflects that the skater is training at a high intensity (anaerobic zone).

DRILLS RECORD SHEET: Aerobic Continuous Stroking with Element Work

Name: _____   Phase: _____   Date: _____

Frequency: 2–3 times per week   Target heart rate training zone: _____   Time period: _____   Body weight

Drill Name	Mode, Elements	Set #	Duration	Heart Rate		
1. Aerobic	On-ice stroking		20–30 minutes	70–85%	0	0
1-a. Counterclockwise	Forward perimeter. Forward crossovers (right over left) on ends, right (RFI edge) to left (LBI edge) mohawk, backward crossover left over right, right back outside edge stretch – hold, backward right over left crossover, left back outside edge stretch – hold, step forward on right forward inside edge for crossover on end (right over left).	1	2½ minutes			
1-b. Clockwise	Forward perimeter. Forward crossovers (left over right) on ends, left (LFI edge) to right (RBI edge) mohawk, backward crossover right over left, left back outside edge stretch – hold, backward left over right crossover, right back outside edge stretch – hold, step forward on left inside edge for crossovers on end (left over right)	2	2½ minutes		0	

1-c. Counterclockwise	backward perimeter. Backward crossovers (left over right) on ends, backward spiral (alternating free-leg/skating leg on each lap) holding a spiral from blue line to blue line, backward crossovers (left over right) on ends, landing position held from blue line to blue line on opposite length/side of spiral – each lap, backward crossovers (left over right) on ends.	3	2½ minutes	0
1-d. Clockwise	Backward perimeter. Backward crossovers (right over left) on ends, backward swizzle-swizzle-swizzle-dip jumps from blue line to blue line (dip jumps can be substituted with cross strokes, or power pulls on one or two legs), backward crossovers (right over left) on ends (crossovers on the ends can be substituted for more difficult steps from Moves in the Field), repeat the same exercise on this length as the previous length skated, backward crossovers (right over left) on ends or substituted steps.	4	2½ minutes	0

(continued overleaf)

DRILLS RECORD SHEET: Aerobic Continuous Stroking with Element Work *(continued)*

Drill Name	Mode, Elements	Set #	Duration	Heart Rate	Recovery Time
1. Aerobic	On-ice stroking		20–30 minutes	70–85%	0
1-e. Forward Power Circles	Skating around a red hockey circle slow crossovers – 8 counts per complete crossover/ 4 counts per stroke, change to fast count of crossovers – 2 counts per complete crossover/ 1 count per stroke. This is done for 1minute 15 seconds slow, 1 minute 15 seconds fast counterclockwise. Repeat the same skating clockwise for a total of 4 sets = 5 minutes in duration.	5		5 minutes or 4 sets of 1¼-minute intervals	
1-f. Backward Power Circles	Skating around a red hockey circle slow crossovers – 8 counts per complete crossover/ 4 counts per stroke, change to fast count of crossovers – 2 counts per complete crossover/ 1 count per stroke. This is done for 1 minute 15 seconds slow, 1 minute 15 seconds fast counterclockwise. Repeat the same skating clockwise for a total of 4 sets = 5 minutes in duration.	6		5 minutes or 4 sets of 1¼-minute intervals	

Note: More advanced skaters can do nonstop footwork in place of the fast set of crossovers. For backward perimeter, back crossovers on ends, dip jumps, cross-in-fronts, cross strokes, or power pulls on long stretch may be added.

Alternating crossover: back outside edge-stretch can be substituted to replace the more difficult or technical skills on the long stretches.

Must remain in target heart rate zone. Cool down 5 minutes by light to moderate stroking on-ice, with total-body flexibility stretching off-ice for 10 minutes.

DRILLS RECORD SHEET: Anaerobic-Simulated Program or Kill Drill

Name: _____   Phase: _____   Time period: _____   Date: _____

Frequency: 2–3 times per week   Target heart rate training zone: _____   Body weight: _____

Drill Name	Mode, Elements	Set #	Duration	Heart Rate	Recovery Time
1. Anaerobic kill drill	On-ice stroking			85–95%	
	1-a. Perform the stroking from the aerobic continuous drill.				
	1-b. Add jumps or combinations at each end and stroking forward or backward to the other end of jump.* Skater can mix up direction and vary the pattern. Must be skating nonstop and jumping at each end. The skater must do three of each jump Scores: the skater gets one point per double, two points per triple, two points per two double combination, three points for triple and double combination, and four points for two triple combinations.	1	2–4 minutes Some skaters may take much longer to complete depending upon beginning anaerobic capacity. Keep track of times, and over a period of time the duration to complete drill should go down dramatically!		1–2 minutes
	1-c. Skating nonstop until drill is completed consisting of jumps on the ends of the arena, doing three of each and starting from easiest in freeskating		Duration may vary as some skaters take nine minutes to complete and some finished in four minutes		

program to the hardest (jump combinations must be integrated!) Skating in between the jumps must be continuous and can be replicated to set up patterns from freeskating programs.

Keeping score with a point system can motivate the skater and keeps them aware of their consistency level.

Scores: The skater receives one point per jump landed and two for a jump combination. If the skater does three double jumps in a row they would receive three points. If the skater can do double jumps, give them one point per jump landed and two points per combination, three for a three jump combination. If the skater can successfully complete triple jumps, the points go up to two points per triple landed and for a triple-double combination they receive 2+1=3 points. If they can successfully do a triple-triple combination they would receive 2+2=4 points.

If your skater can successfully do only double jumps, start with 3 axels, 3 double salchows, 3 double toe-loops, 3 double loops, 3 double flips, 3 double lutz's and 3 double axels. Start with combinations after all the double jumps have been attempted.

(continued overleaf)

DRILLS RECORD SHEET: Anaerobic-Simulated Program or Kill Drill *(continued)*

Drill Name	Mode, Elements	Set #	Duration	Heart Rate	Recovery Time
1. Anaerobic kill drill	On-ice stroking			85–95%	
2. Repeat		2	2–4 minutes		1–2 minutes
3. Repeat		3	2–4 minutes		1–2 minutes
4. Repeat		4	2–4 minutes		1–2 minutes

* This is done with the skater's easiest jump to hardest. Example—the skater can do double lutz-double toe: start with an axel, double salchow, double toe, double loop, double flip, double lutz, then combinations from freeskate program. This could equal 36 jump attempts including 3 jump combinations from free program.

Totals: _____

Note: This structure can be repeated based on progression of conditioning and technical ability. Can repeat the aerobic drill attempting jumps that are technically difficult for the skater; however, the skater has to be able to complete the jump. Attempt at the end of each set (three different jumps or jump combinations): this would be skating level and ability specific. For example, skaters working on double axels should attempt or perform double-double combinations; skaters training various triple jumps should attempt double axel combinations, triples they can land relatively consistently, and all double-double combinations. The skater must emphasize a faster stroking rate and footwork sequence. Skaters and coaches can keep score and record heart rates (training sessions). Be specific and perform only the jumps planned in your programs. Some levels of skating may start with double salchow and work up or down depending on the skill level of the skater.

Must remain in target heart rate zone. Cool down 5 minutes by light to moderate stroking on-ice with total-body flexibility stretching off-ice for 15 minutes.

DRILLS DATA SHEET

Date: _____

Name: _____

Phase of season: _____

Drill name: _____

Duration of drill: _____

Resting heart rate: _____ bpm

Start heart rate: _____ bpm

Maximum heart rate: _____ bpm

Aerobic heart rate training zone: _____ bpm   Actual heart rate: _____

Anaerobic heart rate training zone: _____ bpm   Actual heart rate: _____

Recovery time: _____   Heart rate: _____

How did you feel? _____

Intensity of activity: _____

Activity	Data																
	minutes																
	avg. heart rate																
	minutes																
	avg. heart rate																
	minutes																
	avg. heart rate																
	minutes																
	avg. heart rate																
	minutes																
	avg. heart rate																
	minutes																
	avg. heart rate																
	minutes																
	avg. heart rate																
	minutes																
	avg. heart rate																

CHAPTER 7

Testing for Off-Ice and On-Ice Performance

Skaters, strength coaches, on-ice technical coaches, and parents should be aware of the benefits of testing the skater. First, why test the skater? Testing may be used to screen for possible health risks and musculoskeletal problems, assess athletic talent, and recognize specific weaknesses. All in all, testing can provide valuable information to help develop the skater's individual off-ice and on-ice strength and conditioning program, and it can be a motivational tool.

My reasons for testing are twofold: first, to obtain a baseline measurement of the physical characteristics of the skater before beginning off-ice training, and second, to assess the overall program objectives of off-ice training. If we do not test, how do we know if the skater has improved physically? Finally, pre- and posttesting can be a great motivational tool for the skater. The majority of skaters that I have tested look forward to testing. The tests motivate them to make an intense effort; they want to see how well they can test and try to improve. Retesting increases their motivation because skaters are trying hard to perform at their best. Skaters love the retest or posttest to see, hopefully, improvement in their scores. Overall, testing allows the strength coach and the technical skill coach to gain a basic understanding of the physical characteristics (i.e., strength, power, endurance, and flexibility) of the skater so that appropriate supplemental or skill-training decisions may be applied.

So what tests need to be implemented for the figure skater? To begin with, skaters should be prescreened by a general physician before beginning any type of sport or strenuous exercise off-ice. Although detailing a physical exam for the skater is beyond the scope of this book, it is extremely important to obtain clearance from a doctor before beginning a training program. This exam determines if the athlete has any underlying, serious medical conditions or injuries that could cause problems for that athlete once he or she starts training.

Overall, testing should be practical and functional and should meet the needs of the skater and coach. This chapter provides any technical or strength coach with the ability to measure and evaluate any skater in a field test environment. Keep in mind that these are basic field tests to assess if the objectives of a skater's off-ice strength, power, and conditioning training are being met. These tests are not for scientific research; they are used at various times during the skater's training and competitive season. Obviously, testing can be individualized; however, the initial test should generally be administered in the early off-season and a midtest performed in the early preseason. I also recommend a final post-test before the competitive season (see Chapter 8 on periodization).

The following tests may be used for evaluating the figure skater:

1. Body Weight. Body weight can be measured on a standard medical weight scale. Body weight data is important to use with other testing data, such as vertical jump power and upper body power, to base the results relative to body weight.

2. Body Height. Body height can be measured on a standard weight scale with a height marker, or use a tape measure to record height while the skater stands erect against a wall. Measuring body height is important for tracking the young skater during times of accelerated growth. Measurements can monitor any injuries from on-ice training and plateaus in jump performance or skill work due to bone growth.

3. Girth Measurement. Girth or diameter of the arms, chest, abdominals/waist, hips/buttocks, thighs, and calves is measured using a tape measure. Girth measurements are used to determine if the skater has increased in muscle size. This would be more important for the lean male skater who wants to increase muscle mass. Also, male pairs skaters and ice dancers would probably utilize girth measurements to track their muscle size.

4. Body Composition. Skinfold measurements determine the relative weight of body fat to lean mass (muscles). Measuring the relative weight of fat to muscle accurately monitors loss of body fat. This measurement would be important for the skater who, with the knowledge of his or her coach, wants to decrease some body fat.

5. Flexibility. The sit-n-reach test is used for assessing hamstring/low back flexibility.

6. Ankle Rocker Balance. This field test uses an ankle rocker to determine how long a skater can balance on a single leg.

7. Muscular Strength. Muscular strength is determined by the force that a muscle group can exert against a resistance. Skaters can test muscular strength by performing pull-ups, push-ups, back squats, or the bench press for a designated number of repetitions, usually three to five repetitions. This is an estimated repetition maximum test, projecting what the skater would be able to lift if he or she were performing a one-repetition (1 RM) test. The reason for performing a three- to five-repetition estimated maximum test is that it is safer for the athlete because the load is lighter compared to the 1 RM test.

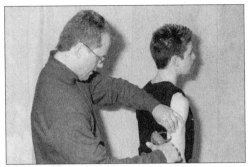

BODY COMPOSITION SKINFOLD TEST
A skater is being assessed for body composition. The strength coach is measuring skinfold thickness with a skinfold caliper at the triceps area; he pinches the skin and reads the measurement of the skinfold.

SIT-N-REACH FLEXIBILITY TEST
The skater is using the sit-n-reach box to assess hamstring/lower back flexibility. Note how the skater is in a pike position: legs straight and together on the floor, knees extended. The skater is leaning forward, pushing the marker down on the box to record the range of motion.

ANKLE ROCKER BALANCE
This test assesses single-leg balance on the ankle rocker. Note how the skater is on the left leg, with the foot placement in the middle of the ankle rocker. The objective of the test is to balance for a duration of time, without allowing the opposite foot or the heel or toe of the tested leg to touch the floor. The timer stops if the skater falls off the ankle rocker or the heel or toe of the tested leg touches the floor (see Chapter 4 for balance training with the ankle rocker).

PULL-UP TEST
A preliminary-level skater is being assessed for upper body muscular strength by performing pull-ups. The total number of technically correct pull-ups is recorded.

ONE-MINUTE TIMED CRUNCH OR CURL-UP TEST
The skater is being tested for local muscular endurance of the abdominal area. Note the body positioning of the skater, with legs over a bench, knee and hip at ninety degrees, and arms crossed at the chest. The objective is to perform as many technically correct crunches in a sixty-second (one-minute) time period. The shoulder blades must be completely off the floor; arms must remain crossed at the chest. The skater then returns to the start position.

DOUBLE-LEG VERTICAL JUMP
Here the skater is being measured for average power by performing a double-leg takeoff vertical jump. This jump test can be performed next to a wall: the skater stands tall with arms fully extended and marks the wall with the tip of the middle finger, using chalk or a marker. The difference between the jump height and reach height (which would be the standing position, arms, hands, and fingers fully extended) determines the total vertical jump of the skater, which can be measured with a tape measure. Note the leg and arm extension of the skater to maximize jump height.

MEDICINE BALL SHOT
The skater is performing a medicine ball shot to measure upper body power. Note the start position with the medicine ball: hands on the ball, arms in, back flat against the wall, legs straight and angled outward. The throw is an explosive push of the arms outward where the skater throws the ball up and out. The distance of the throw is recorded. Note that the back must remain flat against the wall; all the motion must come from the arms extended out. It is more effective to throw the ball up and out, not just straight out.

8. Local Muscular Endurance. This tests the capacity of a muscle or group of muscles to perform continuous movements or contractions against a light resistance or (body weight or weight bar) load over an extended period of time, resisting fatigue, such as one-minute timed sit-ups, a modified crunch test, or push-ups.

9. Anaerobic Power (AP). This tests the amount of work performed utilizing anaerobic or stored energy. AP reflects any type of maximal explosive movement, such as a vertical jump (dynamic and static), long jump, single-leg takeoff jumps, or throwing a four-pound medicine ball from the chest while in a seated position with shoulders against the wall, demonstrating upper body power.

10. Resting Heart Rate. Morning resting heart rate may be assessed at various periods throughout the yearly training cycle to monitor cardiovascular and/or physiological responses and/or stress. Important training time points would be during the preseason and in-season or during times of intense training or competition. For a majority of skaters, September through regionals is a period of great stress due not only to intense on-ice and off-ice training but also stress from other sources, such as starting back to school and stress from peers, family, and extracurricular activities.

11. Skating-Specific Cardiovascular Endurance. This test covers both aerobic and anaerobic energy systems and assesses the skater's conditioning specific to an all-out effort of the long free-skate program.

Keep in mind that the majority of these tests are simple field tests that the technical coach and off-ice strength coach can use to assess skaters. I must reemphasize that the figure skater should be medically screened before beginning on-ice and off-ice training. Second, skaters should be assessed for more detailed musculoskeletal problems through their local orthopedic specialist or sport medicine physician. This can be a valuable evaluation for the skater and technical coach and can complement the strength coach's off-ice program design. The orthopedic or sports medicine physician will be able to evaluate and determine probable sites of common injuries and areas of muscular imbalance for that particular skater.

Before I test skaters or begin off-ice strength and conditioning training, I require them to fill out a Skating and Injury History form (see form on page 137). The skater's training history and injury history play an important role in the testing phase and program design. This form can help coaches obtain a general idea of the skater's training volume on-ice (if his or her on-ice training volume was very high, this would affect how much off-ice training that athlete could initially handle), what skills the skater is training on-ice, if he or she is doing any extensive off-ice training, and if there are general injuries that would contraindicate off-ice training exercises. All this information would be helpful in the initial program design for the skater. On page 139 is a sample athlete off-ice test data sheet for all levels of skaters; however, not all these tests may apply or even be appropriate for various levels of skaters. For example, I do not typically perform body girths and body composition tests for the younger, lower-level skater (preliminary through intermediate levels). Also, certain strength tests, such as the 1 to 10 RM (repetition maximum) back squat and bench press, should be used with caution, especially with the prepubescent figure skater. Technique must be emphasized and fine-tuned prior to testing.

Start position.   **Finish position.**

SINGLE-LEG VERTICAL JUMP

Here the skater is being measured for single-leg takeoff power. The start position shows the jump takeoff start position, off the left leg with the right foot/leg off the floor. The finish position shows the peak height of the skater's jump, with the skater fully extending the arm, hand, and fingers to mark the wall with the right finger. Note the full extension of the skater's body to maximize jump height. The skater would then repeat the same test, jumping off the right leg.

FREE-SKATE PROGRAM HEART RATE TEST

This photo shows a long program heart rate monitor test of a skater. This actual performance was done at an exhibition with judges present to simulate a competitive environment. Start heart rate, maximal heart rate, and average heart rate data was collected. Also, notes were taken on what jumps and elements were attempted, and what elements or jumps were completed or missed.

SKATING AND INJURY HISTORY

Name: _____ Age: _____

Years skating: _____ Test level: _____ Competitive level:_____

On-ice coach:_____

Number of days/week of on-ice training:_____

Number of hours/day of on-ice training: _____

Previous off-ice training:

_____

_____

_____

Skating-related injuries and treatments:

_____

_____

_____

Which of these jumps can you consistently complete? Indicate S for single, D for double, or T for triple.

_____ Waltz jump   _____ Flip jump   _____ Toe loop/Toe walley jump

_____ Lutz jump   _____ Loop jump   _____ Axel jump

_____ Salchow jump   _____ Walley jump (check if skater can complete a walley)

Figure-skating performance goals for the next year:

_____

_____

_____

ATHLETE DATA SHEET

Date/Time: _____   Age: _____

Name: _____   Weight: _____lbs.

Level: _____   Height: _____ins.

Coach: _____

_____

_____

_____

_____

_____

_____

_____

_____

_____

_____

_____

_____

_____

_____

_____

_____

_____

_____

_____

_____

ASSESSMENTS

Body Girths

1. Biceps _____ ins.

2. Chest _____ ins.

3. Abdomen _____ ins.

4. Buttocks _____ ins.

5. Thigh _____ ins.

6. Calf _____ ins.

Body Composition

1. Fat _____

2. LBM _____ lbs.

3. Fat wt _____ lbs.

Flexibility

1. Sit-n-reach _____ ins.

Power

1. Vertical jump power (dynamic) rh _____ jh _____ VJ = _____ ins.

2. Vertical jump (static) rh _____ jh _____ VJ = _____ ins.

3. Single-leg takeoff (left leg) _____ ins.

4. Single-leg takeoff (right leg) _____ ins.

5. Medicine ball shot _____ ft./ins.

Muscular Strength

1. Pull-ups _____

2. 1–10 RM back squat _____ lbs.

3. 1–10 RM bench press _____ lbs.

Muscular Endurance

1. Push-ups (1 min.) _____

2. Sit-ups (1 min.) _____

Ankle Rocker Balance

1. Right leg _____ mins./secs.

2. Left leg _____ mins./secs.

(continued overleaf)

ASSESSMENTS *(continued)*

Long Program (Freeskate) Endurance

1. Resting HR _____ bpm   Target HR zone: Aerobic _____ bpm

2. Program start HR _____ bpm   Target HR zone: Anaerobic _____ bpm

3. Program max HR _____ bpm

4. Age max HR _____ bpm

Comments:

_____

_____

_____

_____

_____

_____

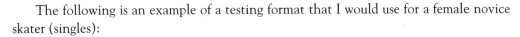

The following is an example of a testing format that I would use for a female novice skater (singles):

1. The skater fills out a skating and injury history questionnaire along with an informed consent form. Depending on the age of the skater, I recommend that the parent attend and discuss various aspects of the skater's background.
2. A resting heart rate is obtained.
3. The strength coach discusses the skater's background and skating goals, goes over any previous injuries, and describes what tests the skater will perform.
4. Body weight, body height, body girth, and body composition are taken. Again, body girths and body composition may be optional, depending on the needs of the athlete. A lot of times the coach will request, along with the skater, to have a girth or body composition measurement taken.
5. The skater performs a brief warm-up with flexibility stretching.
6. The skater is tested on the sit-n-reach for flexibility.
7. The skater is tested on all power tests (VJ, SVJ, single-leg jumps, and upper body power).
8. The skater is tested on pull-ups for upper body strength. (Depending on the skater's level, age, and ability, any 1 to 10 RM strength tests, such as hang cleans, push-presses, back squats, and bench presses, should be tested just after the power tests in number 7.)
9. The skater is tested on one-minute timed sit-ups for local muscular endurance.
10. The skater is tested on one-minute timed push-ups for local muscular endurance.
11. The skater is tested on the ankle rocker.
12. The skater performs total-body flexibility stretches before leaving.
13. On a separate day, the skater will perform her competition long program with the heart rate monitor. Start heart rate, maximal heart rate, and average heart rate will be recorded, as well as any notes on attempted jumps or skills or missed or completed elements.

At this point notes or comments should be written regarding the testing experience. Sometimes I have the singles skater perform some dryland rotation jumps (single loop, axel, double loop, double axel) to get a look at jumping mechanics and body alignment, strength, power, and control on the floor.

Finally, it is important for the off-ice coach to meet with or communicate with the on-ice coach to discuss additional physical needs of the skater. For example, the on-ice coach may mention that the skater lacks an adequate off-ice prepractice warm-up routine. Also, since the technical coach knows the athlete better and has spent more skill-training time with that athlete, the coach may communicate additional information on weaknesses or strengths. For example, I have had numerous coaches tell me that an athlete they were coaching had a weakness with jumping or exploding off the ice; thus, there was a need for increasing vertical height or power of takeoff for these particular skaters. I also make it a point to see the skater train on-ice. I feel that it is helpful for the off-ice strength coach to see what skills that skater is training on-ice, which may add to that skater's overall off-ice training program design.

CHAPTER 8

Periodization: A Skater's Yearly Plan

W e have described in Chapters 2, 3, 4, 5, and 6 all physical components of a figure skater's yearly off-ice training. This, combined with the skater's on-ice skill training, choreography work, and program work, adds up to a lot of components that a skater incorporates into his or her overall training. To fully maximize training potential the skater and coach must have a plan for training all these components.

When should the skater be in the best physical condition within the whole training year? A majority of the competitive figure skaters that I have trained want to be at a physical peak for regionals, sectionals, or nationals.[1] I have had skaters who reached a peak and then had to maintain their physical conditioning throughout a one- to two-month period, such as peaking for regionals and maintaining this through sectionals and nationals. For nonqualifying skaters (preliminary and prejuvenile), the most important competition time period may run from August to September (and regionals for the prejuvenile skater); therefore, they would want to be in their best physical condition at that time. These nonqualifying competitions play an important role; these skaters want to perform a good program to prepare for the future when they will be qualifying at regionals. Thus, like the juvenile- through senior-level skater, these lower-level skaters want to be in top physical condition at this time period.

If a skater can determine when he or she wants to be at a physical peak, how does he or she organize his or her training throughout the training year? *Periodization* is a plan for structuring an athlete's training into various phases or periods, while varying program components as well as training variables, such as volume, intensity, duration, and rest, to achieve peak levels of fitness for the most important competitive time period.

There are three important cycles of training for the athlete. First is the *mesocycle* for figure skating, which can range from one to three months. The mesocycle is a breakdown of training periods, such as off-season, preseason, and in-season (see Tables 8.1 and 8.2). The mesocycle should be organized according to all competitions planned. Second is the *macrocyle,* which consists of a one-year plan. Tables 8.3, 8.4, and 8.5 are sample training and competitive macrocycles. Tables 8.4 and 8.5 provide periodized yearly training and competitive outlines for the novice-, junior-, and senior-level qualifying skater with recommended frequency, volume, intensity, and training modes. There are also recommendations for when the athlete should taper off for competition, which is extremely important. The skater can look at each month to determine what component (strength and/or plyometric) is emphasized. Finally, recommendations for on-ice training components are listed and periodized for the skater. Keep in mind, however, that these tables are general models; skaters need to individualize their own macrocycles based on their requirements and the competitions for which they must peak.

The third cycle is the *microcycle,* which consists of one to two weeks of planned training. The microcycle is important for the skater traveling to an international, when competitions are back to back or close together, or when the skater's off-ice and on-ice training requires quick variation for performance. Figure 8.1 is an example of a one-week microcycle variation of a skater's training including volume and intensity.

Periodization is also used to prevent overtraining. I feel strongly that without a periodized approach to both on-ice skill training and off-ice strength and conditioning training, skaters run the risk of overtraining, which can result in a poorer performance and possibly a higher incidence of skating-related injury.

Periodization of training should incorporate the following:

1. On-ice skill training (learning new elements: jumps, spins, pair lifts, choreography movements, and so on)
2. On-ice program work or program run-throughs
3. On-ice conditioning training or power stroking; simulated program drills for endurance conditioning
4. Off-ice strength and conditioning training, including periodizing the following components: strength training, jump/plyometric training, and endurance conditioning

Note that the warm-up and cool-down programs with flexibility stretching were not mentioned under the off-ice periodized components. Skaters should perform their warm-up and cool-down programs year-round without much variation in volume and intensity.

For periodization to be effective, the skater (with help from the coach) must know when to change or alter training variables. What are all the training variables? The following section lists and defines all the variables that need to be manipulated to promote a physical peak in performance and prevent overtraining.

TABLE 8.1	ONE-YEAR PERIODIZATION TRAINING SCHEDULE
	FOR JUVENILE AND INTERMEDIATE SKATERS

Transition or Active Rest (2–4 weeks)

Purpose: To recover physiologically and psychologically from the in-season competitive phase (overuse or skating-related injuries including muscle fatigue, psychological fatigue, and so on)

Flexibility: Several times daily, prepractice warm-up, postpractice cool-down (additional ballet classes, and so on)

Aerobic Conditioning: Cross-train, emphasizing physical activity in other sports

Anaerobic Conditioning: None

Strength Training: 2 times per week

Plyometrics: None

Other: Skate 2–5 times per week to maintain abilities as desired; review past season and develop goals for next season; search for new music

Early Off-Season (6–7 weeks)

Purpose: To develop strength and aerobic base

Flexibility: Several times daily, prepractice warm-up, postpractice cool-down (additional ballet classes, and so on)

Aerobic Conditioning: Continuous activity at 70–85% MAX HR, 3–5 times/week for 10–15 minutes

Anaerobic Conditioning: None

Strength Training: 3 times per week

Plyometrics: None

Other: Set future goals and master calendar; begin to learn new moves; choose final music; off-ice dance classes to improve presentation; increase knowledge of nutrition

Late Off-Season (10 weeks)

Purpose: To increase strength, begin power base, power and aerobic conditioning, begin anaerobic training

Flexibility: Several times daily, prepractice warm-up, postpractice cool-down (additional ballet classes, and so on)

Aerobic Conditioning: 1–2 times per week at 70–85% MAX HR for 10–15 minutes

(continued overleaf)

145

TABLE 8.1 *(continued)*

Anaerobic Conditioning: 1–2 times per week at 85–95% MAX HR (see Interval Training Schedule); this conditioning can be done on-ice with program run-throughs

Strength Training: 2–3 times per week

Plyometrics: 1 time per week

Other: Further develop and improve new moves; begin to set program to music; continue dance presentation; incorporate sport psychology skills into practice sessions

Preseason (10–14 weeks)

Purpose: Emphasis on sport-specific training, peak levels in skills training, strength, power, endurance conditioning

Flexibility: Several times daily, prepractice warm-up, postpractice cool-down (additional ballet classes, and so on)

Aerobic Conditioning: 1 time per week

Anaerobic Conditioning: 2–3 times per week at 95% MAX HR (see Interval Training Schedule); this conditioning can be done on-ice with program run-throughs

Strength Training: 1–2 times per week

Plyometrics: 1 time per week

Other: Refine choreography on-ice; design costume; begin to run through complete program, sport psychology skills applied to completing program each time

In-Season (12–18 weeks)

Purpose: To maintain strength, power, aerobic, anaerobic conditioning throughout season

Flexibility: Several times daily, prepractice warm-up, postpractice cool-down (additional ballet classes, and so on)

Aerobic Conditioning: None

Anaerobic Conditioning: 2–3 times per week at 95% MAX HR (see Interval Training Schedule); this conditioning can be done on-ice with program run-throughs

Strength Training: 2 times per week

Plyometrics: 1 time per week

Other: Constantly refine and improve program choreography and additional new moves; develop nutritional knowledge for meals while traveling and precompetition; improve sport psychology skills for focus and program performance

TABLE 8.2 OFF-ICE STRENGTH AND JUMP/PLYOMETRIC YEARLY TRAINING CYCLE FOR JUVENILE AND INTERMEDIATE SKATERS

Competition Schedule	Months/Season	On-ice training	Strength-training frequency	Intensity of strength training[a]	Jump and plyometric frequency	Intensity of plyometric training[b]
Transition or Active Rest	Jan./Feb.	Active rest after natls.; work on ideas for new programs and on new elements	None after nationals; 1–2 times per week (Jan.); 2 times in Feb.	Low	0	0
	March	Work on new programs; develop new elements	3 times per week	Light	0	0
	April	Finish new programs; develop new elements	3 times per week	Light	0	0
	May	Finish new programs; develop new elements	2–3 times per week	Light/moderate	0	0
Select Competitions	June	Run through programs	2 times per week	Light/moderate	1 time per week	Light
Select Competitions	July	Go through programs; start to run back-to-back programs	2 times per week	Light/moderate	1 time per week	Light
Select Competitions	August	Same as July	1–2 times per week	Moderate/high	1 time per week	Light/moderate
Select Competitions	September	Refine program; back-to-back run-throughs; intense training	1–2 times per week	Moderate/high	1 time per week	Moderate
Regionals	October	Same as Sept.; refine programs; intense training; taper[c] for regionals	2 times per week; taper for regionals	High	1 time per week with taper	High

a. Intensity of strength exercises is based on volume and intensity; volume = sets X reps; intensity = amount of resistance lifted. Refer to chapters on basic guidelines for off-ice strength and plyometric training.

b. Intensity of plyometrics is based on: 1. Foot contacts of each drill. (total number of jumps on the ground/floor). 2. Amplitude or intensity of each drill: example, double-leg or single-leg jumps. Box heights 12 inches versus 18 inches.

c. Taper is defined as a reduction in frequency and volume of training for physical restoration. Taper according to competition dates.

SPECIFICITY OR EXERCISE CHOICE, ORDER, AND SPEED OF EXERCISE OR LIFT

Movement

Movement is specificity or the mechanical similarity between a training activity and a sport skill. Prioritizing the type of exercises or drills employed during a typical training session and the order in which they are implemented is important. During specific times of training, such as preseason or in-season, a program with strength and power training should emphasize exercises or lifts that require fast or explosive movements.

On-ice: The program could work a particular sequence of double jumps, progress to triple jumps, then progress to footwork drills with jumps. For conditioning purposes, the skater would use continuous aerobic on-ice conditioning or stroking patterns, as suggested in Chapter 6, to build his or her aerobic base. Finally, the skater would progress to kill drills or anaerobic interval training, which would include stroking patterns with jumps in the corners, again as listed in Chapter 6. This example of a program shows how exercise modes or choices can go from general to specific while prioritizing the skating-specific drills for endurance conditioning.

TABLE 8.3   ONE-YEAR PERIODIZATION TRAINING SCHEDULE FOR NOVICE, JUNIOR, AND SENIOR SKATERS

Transition or Active Rest (2–4 weeks)

Purpose: To recover physiologically and psychologically from the in-season competitive phase (overuse or skating-related injuries including muscle fatigue, psychological fatigue, and so on)

Flexibility: Several times daily, prepractice warm-up, postpractice cool-down (additional ballet classes, and so on)

Aerobic Conditioning: Cross-train, emphasizing physical activity in other sports

Anaerobic Conditioning: None

Strength Training: 2 times per week

Plyometrics: None

Other: Skate 2–5 times per week to maintain abilities as desired; review past season and develop goals for next season; search for new music

Early Off-Season (6–8 weeks)

Purpose: To develop strength and aerobic base

Flexibility: Several times daily, prepractice warm-up, postpractice cool-down (additional ballet classes, and so on)

Aerobic Conditioning: Continuous activity at 70–85% MAX HR, 3–5 times/week for 30 minutes

Anaerobic Conditioning: None

Strength Training: 3 times per week

Plyometrics: None

Other: Set future goals and master calendar; begin to learn new moves; choose final music; off-ice dance classes to improve presentation; increase knowledge of nutrition

Late Off-Season (10 weeks)

Purpose: To increase strength, begin power base, power and aerobic conditioning, begin anaerobic training

Flexibility: Several times daily, prepractice warm-up, postpractice cool-down (additional ballet classes, and so on)

Aerobic Conditioning: 1–2 times per week at 70–85% MAX HR for 30 minutes

Anaerobic Conditioning: 2–3 times per week at 85–95% MAX HR (see Interval Training Schedule)

Strength Training: 2–3 times per week

Plyometrics: 2 times per week

Other: Further develop and improve new moves; begin to set program to music; continue dance presentation; incorporate sport psychology skills into practice sessions

Preseason (8–10 weeks)

Purpose: Emphasis on sport-specific training, peak levels in skills training, strength, power, endurance conditioning

Flexibility: Several times daily, prepractice warm-up, postpractice cool-down (additional ballet classes, and so on)

Aerobic Conditioning: 1 time per week

Anaerobic Conditioning: 2–3 times per week at 95% MAX HR (see Interval Training Schedule)

Strength Training: 1–2 times per week

Plyometrics: 1–2 times per week

Other: Refine choreography on-ice; design costume; begin to run through complete program; sport psychology skills applied to completing program each time

In-Season (12–18 weeks)

Purpose: To maintain strength, power, aerobic, anaerobic conditioning throughout season

Flexibility: Several times daily, prepractice warm-up, postpractice cool-down (additional ballet classes, and so on)

(continued overleaf)

TABLE 8.3 *(continued)*

Aerobic Conditioning: None

Anaerobic Conditioning: 2–3 times per week at 95% MAX HR, (see Interval Training Schedule); this conditioning can be done on-ice with program run-throughs

Strength Training: 2 times per week

Plyometrics: 1 time per week

Other: Constantly refine and improve program choreography and additional new moves; develop nutritional knowledge for meals while traveling and precompetition; improve sport psychology skills for focus and program performance

---

Off-ice: The program could utilize basic strength exercises in the off-season to obtain a base strength adaptation (back squats, lunges, standing military press), then progress to more technical multijoint core strength and power exercises, which also require high-velocity techniques in the preseason and in-season (hang pulls, hang cleans, push press, jerk press, plyometric drills such as single-leg jumps, sport cord drills).

Volume

Volume is the amount of training or total amount of work done per training session. Volume may be determined by the total number of repetitions accomplished in a training session.

On-ice: Volume would include the total number of double or triple jumps performed in one freestyle session, or the total number of pairs or dance lifts completed per session.

Off-ice: Volume includes the total number of repetitions with various loads for a strength exercise; for example, performing 3 sets of 10 repetitions (30 total repetitions) of back squats with 45 pounds. The volume totals 1,350 pounds.

Intensity

Intensity is the power output of an exercise or training session. In simple terms, intensity may be described as the difficulty of training, which depends on the load (amount of weight lifted per repetition) and the speed of movement of the exercise. Intensity may be determined by heavy, moderate, and light training.

Figure 8.1 represents how skaters can vary their training of volume and intensity on a weekly basis. This bar graph charts the training variables of intensity (light gray bars) and volume (dark gray bars) during a one-week microcycle. Note that volume is moderate on Monday and Tuesday, begins to drop off on Wednesday and Thursday, and by Friday is low. Intensity begins high on Monday and drops off on Tuesday and again on Wednesday. On Thursday, intensity rebounds to near high, but by Friday, intensity, along with volume, is very low. Volume and intensity are varied so that the skater is not training with too high a volume in conjunction with high intensity, with the ultimate goal of maximizing training performance through changing these critical variables. For example, on Wednesday, intensity is very low with volume moderate; on Thursday, volume is moderate and intensity is high. Note that on Friday, when skaters are typically fatigued from a week of training, both volume and intensity are very low, and then finally on Saturday there is complete rest.

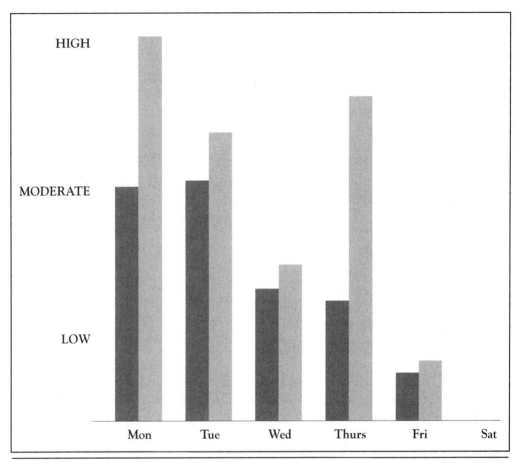

FIGURE 8.1   VARYING INTENSITY AND VOLUME IN A ONE-WEEK MICROCYCLE TRAINING PERIOD

On-ice: Intensity reflects the difficulty of a practice session (for example, double jumps versus triple jumps or jumps versus spins). Also, difficulty of pairs lifts can vary in intensity; for example, a double twist versus a triple twist for pairs skaters. Ice dance skill work intensity can vary with number of program run-throughs, stroking patterns, and working on a short program versus a long program.

Off-ice: Intensity reflects the amount of weight lifted on a strength exercise (for example, lifting 135 pounds on a back squat for 3 sets of 5 reps is a high-intensity strength-training exercise versus 3 sets of 12 reps at 85 pounds, which is low-intensity strength training).

Duration
Duration is the length of a training phase in sessions, days, weeks, or months.

On-ice: Skill work, choreography, and program work duration.

Off-ice: Length of phases or sessions of strength, jump/plyometric, and endurance conditioning; for example, in six weeks of strength training, each session may have forty-five minutes of strength training or thirty minutes of aerobic conditioning.

Frequency

Frequency is the number of specific components or training sessions on a daily, weekly, and monthly basis.

On-ice: Frequency of freestyles, power stroking, moves in the field, and/or pairs or ice dance sessions, such as two freestyles and one power class three days per week.

Off-ice: Frequency of strength, jump/plyometric, or conditioning sessions, such as two strength sessions and one plyometric or conditioning session per week.

Rest

Rest is probably the most important periodization variable, yet is the least utilized by skaters. Rest would include the amount of rest time or recovery between exercises and sets (thirty seconds to three minutes) within a training session or rest between training sessions (twenty-four hours to forty-eight hours).

Off-ice: A proposed weekly rest schedule is

   Monday: off-ice jump/plyometric session
   Tuesday: no off-ice training
   Wednesday: off-ice strength training
   Thursday: no off-ice training
   Friday: off-ice strength training
   Saturday and Sunday: rest

On-ice: There should be rest intervals between technical skills (jumps, spins, lifts, stroking) and between program work or program run-throughs, and also complete rest days of no skating so that the skater can fully recover from on-ice training.

Note: Keep in mind that periodization of volume and intensity is also incorporated into the components of jump/plyometric and endurance-conditioning training (see periodization charts on page 145–153).

TRAINING PHASES: TIMING PERIODIZATION

The timing of periodization program design is important. Each skater and his or her respective coach must determine when the figure skater should peak. Keep in mind that a physical peak in off-ice training, on-ice skill training, and on-ice endurance conditioning may last from one to three or four weeks. Through performance testing of novice, junior, and senior elite figure skaters, I have noticed that physical characteristics (power, muscular strength and endurance, and on-ice heart rate monitoring or heart rate response) were all maintained for a three- to four-week period, from sectionals through the U.S. National Championships.

So how would a skater, with help from the on-ice technical coach and off-ice strength coach, formulate his or her yearly training schedule in order to peak at regionals or a specific time of the competitive season? Figure 8.2 is a training schematic or macrocycle of volume, intensity, and skill training for one year, including the qualifying competitions: regionals, sectionals, and nationals. This model would reflect peaking in October and

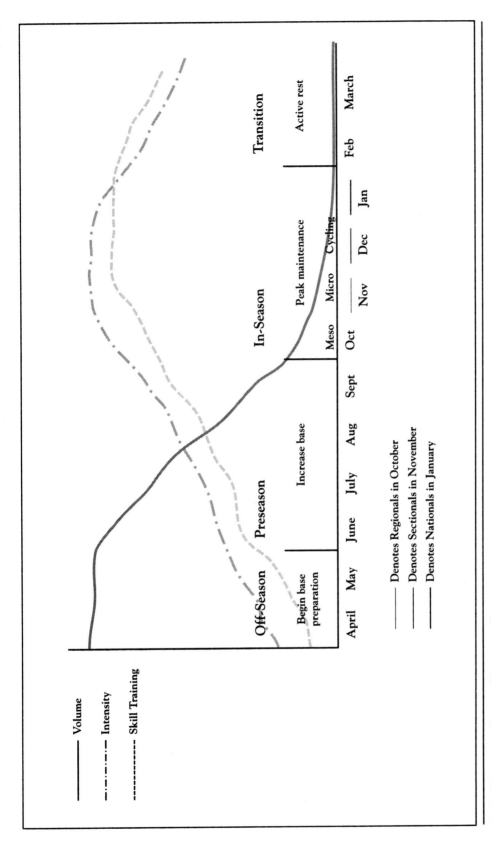

FIGURE 8.2   YEARLY TRAINING SCHEMATIC

TABLE 8.4   Off-Ice Strength and Jump/Plyometric Yearly Training Cycle for Novice, Junior, and Senior Skaters

Competition Schedule	Months/Season	On-ice training	Strength-training frequency	Intensity of strength training[a]	Jump and plyometric frequency	Intensity of plyometric training[b]
Transition or Active Rest	Jan./Feb.	After natls. take a break; work on ideas for new programs and on new elements	None after nationals	Low	0	
Junior Worlds	March	Work on new program and elements	3 times per week	Light/moderate	0	
	April	Work on new programs and elements	3 times per week	Moderate	1 time per week	
Select Competitions	May	Finish new programs; develop new elements	2 times per week	Moderate	2 times per week	Light
Select Competitions	June	Finish new programs; develop new elements	2–3 times per week	Light	2 times per week	Light
Select Competitions	July	Run through programs; start back-to-back run-throughs	2–3 times per week	Light	2 times per week	Moderate
Select Competitions	August	Same as July	1–2 times per week	Moderate	1–2 times per week	Moderate
	September	Taper[c] for internationals; run through 1 long, 2 short back to back	1–2 times per week	Moderate/high	1–2 times per week	Moderate/high

Competition	Month	Program	Frequency	Intensity	Frequency	Intensity
Regionals/Internationals	October	Same as Sept.; refine programs; intense training; taper for regionals/internationals	2 times per week	Moderate/high	1 time per week with taper	High
Sectionals/Internationals	November	Same as Sept./Oct.; refine programs; intense training; taper for sectionals/internationals	2 times per week	Moderate/high	1 time per week with taper	Moderate/high
Junior Nationals	December	Continued refinement of program; taper to competition	2 times per week	Moderate/high	1 time per week with taper	Moderate/high
Senior National Championship	January	Continued refinement of program; taper to competition	2 times per week	Moderate/high	1 time per week; taper for nationals	High

a. Intensity of strength exercises is based on volume and intensity; volume = sets × reps; intensity = amount of resistance lifted, refer to chapters on basic guidelines for off-ice strength and plyometric training.

b. Intensity of plyometrics is based on: 1. Foot contacts of each drill (total number of jumps on the ground/floor). 2. Amplitude or intensity of each drill: example, double-leg or single-leg jumps. Box heights 12 inches versus 18 inches.

c. Taper is defined as a reduction in frequency and volume of training for physical restoration. Taper according to competition dates.

TABLE 8.5   YEARLY TRAINING CYCLE CARDIO CHART FOR NOVICE, JUNIOR, AND SENIOR SKATERS

Competition Schedule	Months	On-ice training schedule	Number of aerobic sessions per week	Minutes per session	% maximum heart rate	Number of anaerobic sessions	% maximum heart rate
Transition or Active Rest	Jan./Feb.	After nationals take a break; work on new programs, elements, jumps, and spins	Low-level aerobic exercise after nationals	After nationals 15–30 minutes per session	70–85%	0	0
Junior World Camp	March	Work on new programs; show program's new elements, jumps, and spins	3	20–30 minute session	70–85%	0	0
Select Competitions	April	Work on new programs; show program's new elements, jumps, spins	2–3	20–30 minute session	70–85%	0	0
	May	Finish new programs; develop new elements	1–2	20–30 minute session	75–85%	2–3	85–95%
Select Competitions	June	Finish new programs; develop new elements	1–2	20–30 minute session	75–85%	2–3	85–95%
Select Competitions	July	Run through programs back to back	1	20–30 minute session	75–85%	3	85–95%

August		Same as July	1	20–30 minute session	70–85%	3	95%
September	Select Competitions/Internationals	Vary run-through, short/long back-to-back, 5–6 times per week; intense training; taper[a]	1	20–30 minute session	70–85%	3–4	95%
October	Regionals	Same as Sept.; refine programs; intense training; taper	First two weeks: 1 session; last two weeks: 1–0	0	70–85%	2–3	95%
November	Sectionals	Same as Sept./Oct.; refine programs; intense training; taper	No aerobic session[b]	0	0	2–3	95%

a. Taper is defined as a reduction in frequency and volume of training for physical restoration; taper according to competition dates.

b. On-ice conditioning may be substituted as part of the total endurance training. The skater should perform no aerobic component based on the assumption that the skater is performing multiple back-to-back run-throughs.

maintaining this physical peak through January or microcycling to peak twice within this time period.

To further simplify this periodized model, the skater's total training and competitive season is comprised of four separate phases or periods:

1. Transition or active rest
2. Off-season
3. Preseason
4. In-season

Transition or Active Rest Phase

Purpose: To allow the skater to recover physically and psychologically from the in-season or competitive phase. The skater should perform some type of nonskating physical activity not related to typical on-ice skating or off-ice strength, power, and conditioning training. Some examples would be cycling, swimming, and hiking, or team sports, such as soccer and basketball. This is also an ideal time to rest from on-ice skill work and program work. It may be necessary for the highly competitive skater to rest completely for one to two weeks with no physical activity planned for joint/muscle recovery, injury recovery, and mental recovery. Active rest can last anywhere from two to three weeks, depending on the individual skater and his or her physical and psychological condition.

Off-season: Preparatory Phase

Purpose: To build strength and aerobic conditioning base, which prepares the skater's body for the more technical upcoming phases.

  Off-ice:

  Flexibility training. Emphasize proper warm-up with total-body static flexibility training prior to on-ice practice and/or any form of off-ice training. Emphasize cooling down with flexibility stretching after the skater's last on-ice session of the day and after off-ice strength and conditioning training (see Chapter 2).

  Strength training. Perform nonspecific total-body resistance training; volume should be moderate to high, intensity should be low.

  Jump training. Dryland rotations may be performed at low volume, low intensity.

  Endurance conditioning. Skaters should begin work on their aerobic conditioning base (intermediate- to senior-level skater).

  On-ice: Skaters should begin new program work (emphasize choreography) and work on new elements, jumps, and spins. Technical emphasis on-ice should be structured to a low degree of intensity with variation in volume of jumps and pairs and dance lifts.

Preseason: Strength/Power Anaerobic Endurance Phase

Purpose: The beginning of very technical sport-specific training, preparing for the upcoming competition season. In figure skating, the preseason ends with the first competition of the season.

Off-ice:

Strength training. Sport-specific resistance exercises of high volume and low intensity. There can be some microcycles or weekly variations of moderate volume and moderate- to high-intensity training.

Power jump/plyometric training. Begin plyometric training. Dryland jump rotations are continued. Volume is moderate to high; intensity is low.

Endurance conditioning. Aerobic conditioning is reduced. There is a shift into anaerobic or interval endurance conditioning (on-ice power stroking, kill drills).

On-ice: New programs should be completed. Skaters should be completing full program run-throughs. New elements, jumps, spins, pairs, and dance lifts (sport-specific skills) should be thoroughly developed.

In-Season: Maintenance Phase

Purpose: Simply put, the in-season begins with the first competition of the year (regionals, sectionals, or an international) and ends with the last competition of the skating season (could be regionals, sectionals, nationals, or junior nationals or Olympic or world competitions). The overall goal is to maintain physical conditioning and skill levels for the entire competitive season. Since some skaters can have a long in-season, microcycles or weekly variations may be important to achieve a peak in performance at the end of the in-season. Overall, volume of physical training is low while intensity is high for both skill training and physical off-ice training.

Off-ice:

Strength training. Low-volume, high-intensity, sport-specific resistance exercises and multijoint strength/power exercises (hang cleans, jerk presses).

Jump/plyometric training. Low-frequency, low-volume, high-intensity dryland jump drills and plyometric exercises.

Endurance conditioning. On-ice program run-throughs or even modified back-to-back program run-throughs. Low frequency on-ice kill drills or near-maximal interval stroking on-ice.

Tactical circuit training. Low frequency with near-maximal heart rate intensity.

On-ice: Emphasis should be placed on refining the skater's program. Maintenance of skill levels is important. Volume of training on-ice should be low, due to the high-intensity levels of the program run-throughs. Rest days should be implemented for recovery purposes.

To summarize, the outcome goal of periodized training is a peak in physical, skill, and program performance, as well as preventing injuries resulting from overtraining. How many skaters have trained on-ice with increasing intensity without periodizing any variables, such as volume, duration, frequency, or rest? How many skaters have trained hard without a plan, pushing themselves until an overuse injury occurs or technique declined or plateaued (especially during the in-season)? Periodization is a great method to prevent training plateaus and boredom, thus preventing injury. Skaters cannot expect to train on-ice and off-ice with the same volume, intensity, and duration throughout the year without rest periods and expect their performance to peak at the appropriate time and injuries to be held to a minimum. Keep in mind that a juvenile skater may have an entirely different yearly plan compared to a novice-level skater. Overall, the periodized schedule is about change and variation. It is up to the coach and skater to formulate this schedule immediately after the last major competition for the upcoming season. Finally, this plan should consist of realistic goals broken down into certain modes of training, at specific times of the training year, and with a specified frequency and duration within the training year.

The following guideline summarizes periodization. The skater and coach may use this summary as a quick reference to design a periodized program. The summary simplifies the concepts of periodization and presents an actual periodized mesocycle using two strength exercises, one lower body and the other upper body.

SUMMARY OF PERIODIZATION

What is periodization?

Periodization is structured training. The figure skater's training and competition year should be planned to:

- Prevent overreaching and/or overtraining

- Peak physically for on-ice performance at a specific competition time and/or maintain physical peak for a certain time period

How does the figure skater and coach plan for the year?

- Determine what the most important competition or competition period of the year is.

- Structure your off-ice and on-ice supplemental training to peak for this specific competition or time period, such as internationals in September and/or October, sectionals, and nationals, or Olympic or world competitions.

- Schedule the following training phases:

   1. Off-season (early and late)

   2. Preseason

   3. In-season

   4. Transition or active rest

What do you periodize?

The following components and training periods should be periodized.

- Components: Off-Ice
  1. Strength training
  2. Jump/plyometric training
  3. Endurance conditioning (off-ice and on-ice)

- Components: On-Ice
  1. Endurance conditioning (stroking)
  2. Jumps, pairs/dance lifts, program run-throughs

- Training Variables: Off-Ice
  1. Choice of exercise (back squats, push press, and so on)
  2. Volume (total number of repetitions performed per exercise: 3 sets of 10 reps = 30 total repetitions)
  3. Intensity or load (amount of weight lifted to perform a certain number of repetitions: 45 pounds on back squat at $3 \times 10 = 1,350$ pounds total load lifted)
  4. Frequency (number of training sessions per day, week, month)
  5. Duration (total time of the actual training session based on the total number of exercises)
  6. Rest periods (recovery between training sets, exercises, sessions, or days of training)

- Training Variables: On-Ice
  1. Choice of exercise or skill work (endurance stroking or jumps, lifts, and other related elements)
  2. Volume (intervals of stroking, total repetitions of jumps or lifts)
  3. Intensity (heart rate zone of endurance stroking [aerobic or anaerobic], magnitude of jumps [doubles, triples, quads, pairs and dance lifts])
  4. Frequency (number of freestyle endurance sessions per day, week, month)

(continued overleaf)

5. Duration (total time of endurance stroking session, duration of freestyle)

6. Rest periods (rest or recovery between on-ice stroking endurance intervals, jumps on-ice, pairs/dance lifts, freestyle sessions)

How do you periodize?

Periodization is based on:

- *Microcycle:* weekly planning

- *Mesocycle:* one- to three-months' planning

- *Macrocycle:* one-year planning

The figure skater and coach should manage periodization as follows:

- Gradually increase intensity of training

- Decrease volume as intensity increases

- Taper off training prior to major competition

- Implement microcycles when needed

Table 8.6 represents figure-skating periodization training variables for an off-ice strength-training mesocycle.

TABLE 8.6	INDIVIDUAL PHASES IN A ONE- TO TWO-MONTH PERIOD				
	Preparation	*Strength*	*Power*	*Peaking*	*Active Rest*
Sets	3–4	3–5	3–4	2–3	
Reps	10–15	8–12	3–6	2–5	
Volume	High	Medium/high	Low	Very low	
Intensity*	Low	Medium/high	Low	Very low	
Intensity (%)*	70–75	80–85	90–95	95–100	
Rest Periods (Min.)	1	1.5	1.5–2	2–3	
# of Training Weeks	4–6	3–4	2–3	1	

*Intensity equals percentage of the estimated repetition maximum (RM); thus, 1 RM reflects the amount of resistance that is lifted per exercise set.

Table 8.7 is an example of a ten-week (mesocycle) strength-training phase for a figure skater using two major exercises: back squat and bench press. The resistance (pounds) is based on a senior ladies national-level skater, nineteen years of age. Her test results are as follows:

Exercise	Test Results for 1 RM
Back squat	225 pounds
Bench press	115 pounds

TABLE 8.7   TEN-WEEK MESOCYCLE STRENGTH-TRAINING PHASE*

	Exercise	Volume (sets x reps)	Intensity	Rest
Preparation Phase	Back squats	3 × 12	180 pounds	1 minute
(4 weeks)	Bench press	3 × 12	80 pounds	1 minute
Strength Phase	Back squats	3 × 8	205 pounds	1½ minutes
(3 weeks)	Bench press	3 × 8	95 pounds	1½ minutes
Power Phase	Back squats	4 × 4	235 pounds	2 minutes
(2 weeks)	Bench press	4 × 4	105 pounds	2 minutes
Peaking Phase	Back squats	3 × 3	250 pounds	2½ minutes
(1 week)	Bench press	3 × 3	110 pounds	2½ minutes

* Strength training should be performed on alternating days; Monday, Wednesday, Friday or Tuesday, Thursday, Saturday. Assistive strength exercises should be added for overall strength development.

CHAPTER 9

Myths and Truths

Every time I conduct a seminar or develop an off-ice training program for a skater and/or skating club, I stress the importance of involving the technical coach and the parents. One problem with off-ice strength and conditioning training and figure skating is a simple lack of knowledge by the skater, coach, or parent of what off-ice strength and conditioning training is, what purpose it serves, and how to get off-ice training started. It is important, especially for the technical coach, to know the basic terminology, principles, and guidelines of warm-up and cool-down, flexibility training, strength, power, and endurance-conditioning training, and periodization. Over the past nine years, I have noticed a considerable improvement in off-ice training. More skaters are performing off-ice training, rinks and skating programs are building off-ice training facilities, and more coaches want to be educated. However, we could further improve in the following areas:

1. Increasing the number of skaters involved in strength training
2. Getting the grassroots-level skater (preliminary to intermediate) involved in structured off-ice strength and conditioning training
3. Determining the specific needs of each skater: his or her strengths and weaknesses
4. Using more periodized structure
5. Encouraging skaters to properly warm up, stretch, and cool down
6. Improving the balance of aerobic and anaerobic endurance conditioning for the novice-, junior-, and senior-level skater
7. Correctly using jump and plyometric training

8. Keeping communication open with the skater who has a skating-related injury and is still training on-ice

9. Balancing on-ice and off-ice training, especially for prepubescent singles skaters who are attempting a high volume of jumps on-ice in a typical week, month, and year of training

10. Instituting rest periods and rest days for the competitive skater throughout the training year

With the increased technical skill component of skating, be it the emphasis on jump rotations (triples, triple-triple combinations, and quads), pair lifts combined with jumps, or the dynamics of ice dance, off-ice strength and conditioning is no longer an alternative but a *necessity*. Off-ice strength and conditioning training may be a way of prolonging a skater's career by preventing injuries or lessening the severity of injuries.

I have noticed a gap in training among skaters. Only a handful of preliminary- to intermediate-level skaters are performing off-ice strength training; however, at the upper levels skaters are more apt to perform consistent off-ice strength and conditioning training. We need to target our grassroots-level skaters. However, some figure-skating coaches and parents feel that the younger skater is too young to begin resistance training or perform strength/power exercises off-ice. Coaches frequently ask how old a skater must be to begin off-ice training. My basic response is that if a skater, or any athlete performing any sport, can listen to and apply instructions on skill work, he or she is able to perform off-ice training. I have sometimes wondered why younger figure skaters are allowed to perform many jump repetitions on-ice, the impact forces causing stress to their immature, growing bodies, and yet are not allowed to perform off-ice training because it may be "dangerous." The stress of skating itself (jumps, spins, stroking, pair lifts, dance movements) can impact the younger skater, yet these lower-level skaters are usually the ones not properly warming up, cooling down, and stretching or performing progressive strength training.

For higher-level skaters, their training programs need to emphasize physical maintenance and increased endurance conditioning. Here the importance shifts to keeping skaters healthy and free of injury. Remember, the needs analysis should be applied to every skater at every level, and the program design must be *individualized*.

FREQUENTLY ASKED QUESTIONS ABOUT OFF-ICE TRAINING

Why should skaters perform off-ice training? Skaters should perform all components (warm-up and cool-down with flexibility training, strength training, jump and plyometric training, and endurance conditioning) for injury prevention and enhancement of their physical capacity, which will improve their on-ice performance.

How many times per week should the skater be in off-ice strength and conditioning classes or training sessions? The lower-level skater (preliminary to juvenile) should perform off-ice training two to three times per week; the intermediate- to senior-level skater should perform off-ice training three to four times per week. Travel, competitions, and

BACK SQUAT

An eight-year-old preliminary-level skater performs a back squat. Younger skaters can benefit from some of the technical exercises, although their progression needs to be monitored more closely than that of older skaters. This skater is performing the back squat with only nine pounds of resistance. However, when this skater first started off-ice training, she had to demonstrate and progress with performing back squats with just her own body weight; thus, no external resistance was used for an extended period of time. This was due to some of her technique flaws that needed to be mastered, prior to advancement with extra resistance or by adding extra sets, repetitions, an so on. As with any skill acquisition, it is amazing how quickly the younger figure skater progresses with technique of off-ice weight-lifting exercises. These younger athletes are not like the athletes from sports such as soccer, tennis, or swimming. They are already highly skilled athletes due to the nature of learning figure skating skills on-ice, which stimulate the gross and fine motor skill learning patterns at the age these kids begin instruction or just skating.

FRONT SHOULDER PRESS

This preliminary-level skater is performing an upper body (shoulder, upper back, arm, and core stabilizing strengthening) exercise. Again, the resistance for this skater is nine pounds.

school schedules, as well as other extracurricular activities, may affect this frequency. If the figure skater can perform three off-ice training sessions per week on alternate days he or she can optimally adapt.

Is lifting free weights safe for the young (seven- to fourteen-year-old) skater? In my ten years of work training skaters and conducting seminars, this is the most frequently asked question! Yes, off-ice strength training through weight lifting, with a weight bar, weight bar with weight plates, or dumbbells, can be safe and beneficial for prepubescent skaters; however, there are guidelines for their training:

1. These skaters must be instructed and supervised by a qualified, experienced strength coach or trainer.
2. Program design must be appropriate for the skater's maturity level.
3. The skater must be supervised at all times.
4. Appropriate exercise technique has to be emphasized first, then gradual progression with resistances.
5. The program design must include a variety of exercises, and the experience for the child must be fun and encourage him or her to gain strength.

Please keep in mind that there are several associations that have position statements on strength training and the prepubescent athlete (National Strength and Conditioning Association [NSCA], Colorado Springs, Colorado, and the American College of Sports Medicine [ACSM], Indianapolis, Indiana). Coaches, parents, and skaters can research journal articles or look up the actual position statements from both the NSCA and ACSM, or contact each.

National Strength and Conditioning Association: (719) 632-6722,
or Web site: www.nsca-lift.org

American College of Sports Medicine: 1-800-486-5643

Please refer to Chapter 3 for a description of qualified instructors and guidelines for training figure skaters off-ice.

Should the skater perform off-ice training before or after on-ice training? This question is frequently asked by the on-ice skill coach. My answer depends on the following factors:

1. Level and age of the skater (for example, lower-level younger skaters can perform off-ice training prior to taking the ice). Typically, higher-level skaters, mainly novice through senior level, would want to perform their off-ice training after their on-ice training, especially since their overall training structure is more complicated and has more overall training components compared to the lower-level skater.
2. Component of off-ice training scheduled for that day (for example, strength training, jump/plyometric and/or endurance conditioning). It is not recommended that skaters perform any type of endurance (aerobic and anaerobic) conditioning training prior to taking the ice, other than their typical warm-up activity.

3. Volume and intensity of the scheduled workout (for example, low, moderate, or high). A high-intensity workout or definitely high volume or lots of total repetitions in off-ice training is not recommended for the skater that will skate right after off-ice training.

4. Day of the training week (for example, early, midway, or late in the training week). As it gets later in the week (Thursday, Friday, and Saturday), fatigue, especially in the legs, may indicate that the skater should perform off-ice training after skating.

5. What is scheduled for that freestyle, pairs, or dance session (for example, spins, field moves, jump technique, program work, or program run-throughs). For example, if a skater is training a lot of technical jumps, pairs or ice dance lifts on-ice, or program run-throughs, he or she would want to perform off-ice training after practice. On the other hand, if a skater just concentrated on field moves and choreography for a particular day's training, he or she could perform off-ice training prior to taking the ice. To keep this simple, when possible, have the skater perform his or her off-ice training after he or she finishes his or her on-ice training. However, there are situations when performing off-ice training before skating can be helpful. During cycles of jump and plyometric training, it may be beneficial to perform those before skating practice. Actually, these can be a great warm-up for the skater. Overall, the answer to this question is very individualized.

On the downside, I have had to modify my off-ice training program design due to skaters practicing on-ice for extended periods, such as two to three hours, and coming to off-ice class with great physical and mental fatigue. It is very important for the strength coach to recognize this and change the program design for that training day. In this situation, it is advisable for the skater to take in lots of fluids and good-quality food and to emphasize light to moderate strength workouts, balance training, core body training, and, finally, a lot of stretching post workout.

Should the competitive skater continue his or her off-ice training at competitions? This depends on the length of the skater's competitive week. For events (junior world, international, national, world, and Olympics) when travel may be long and the skater is there for at least five to seven days, a light strength and power workout may be necessary. My recommendation would be a strength workout combined with sport cord drills (speed/skill drills such as jump takeoff, landing position check-outs, and arm check-outs). Finally, low-intensity jump training drills may be performed. Performing off-ice workouts while at competitions will also depend on the facility and equipment availability. The skater (especially at internationals) may have to perform strength/resistance exercises using his or her own body weight and sport cords. Overall, the purpose is for the skater to maintain strength and power levels while at these competitions, sustaining his or her physical peak for on-ice competing.

What about the extra cost involved in off-ice training? Is it worth the time and money to schedule off-ice training? Yes. The cost involved in the competitive sport of figure skating is enormous. Nevertheless, off-ice training is an important investment in a skater's career. My objective for each skater that I train is to prolong his or her skating career through off-ice strength and conditioning training.

The question then arises, "Is it a matter of how much ice time the skater has, or is it the balance of his or her on-ice skill training combined with off-ice strength and conditioning training?" I feel that we can create a better figure-skating athlete if we supplement appropriately with off-ice training, and start this at the grassroots level. Obviously, the skater has to skate; he or she must be on the ice. However, is this done in a way in which the skater has time to perform off-ice training yet also has days of complete rest? Are there days when the skater reduces the frequency and duration of training on-ice to get more off-ice time in the weight room? If the coach, parent, and skater sit down and work out a well-balanced schedule, the cost for off-ice training can be accounted for as there won't be extra expenses for extra ice time.

Off-ice training can be cost effective. Skaters can train in small groups with relatively inexpensive free-weight equipment, sport cords, jump ropes, slideboards, jump boxes, medicine balls, and other related equipment.

There are creative ways to establish a sound off-ice program at your training facility. There are some simple exercises that can even be implemented at home. I would not advocate all the skater's off-ice strength and conditioning training to be done at home; however, exercises such as push-ups, chair dips, crunches, sit-ups, sport cord exercises, and slideboard exercises may be done at home with limited space. To summarize, I think the skater, coach, and parent must ask these questions: How do we create a strong, powerful, and well-conditioned athlete? Does the skater need to be on the ice two and a half to three hours per day, five to six days a week and compete six to eight times a year? Or should this skater periodize his or her training; train two hours on-ice on Monday with no off-ice training, then train one and a half hours on-ice on Tuesday but incorporate off-ice strength and conditioning training, and alternate this structure throughout the week. It may be too expensive for a skater to participate in an off-ice strength and conditioning class year-round, but what about the cost for that skater's ice time or competing in a nonqualifying competition, such as off-season competition in the month of March? Perhaps it would be better to let that skater train off-ice versus compete at that time period. Maybe that skater could perform off-ice training if it was budgeted and the whole training year was balanced and structured through periodization.

When skaters perform in too many nonqualifying competitions, this may take away from their total periodized on-ice and off-ice training, not to mention the cost involved in these competitions. I am suggesting that the skater structure the yearly training program both on-ice and off-ice and balance the training and competitive schedule; hopefully this will be cost effective and allow that skater to be a part of an off-ice strength- and conditioning-training program, which will help the skater become a better athlete.

Won't skaters "bulk up" if they lift weights?[1] Numerous skaters, coaches, and parents, especially novice-, junior-, and senior-level female skaters, have asked this question. I feel that the concern about "bulking up" has gone to an extreme and is more a lack of education by the skater, coach, and parent. Keep in mind that bulk may be added to a skater in two ways: by increasing lean body mass (LBM) or by increasing body fat. The female, pubescent, novice to senior skater can certainly add extra body weight, specifically fat

GROUP OFF-ICE STRENGTH TRAINING
A class of skaters performs their strength exercises in the weight room. Within this class, each skater may be on an individualized program. It is highly recommended that the group size be limited to six skaters per instructor for appropriate supervision and instruction.

GROUP OFF-ICE JUMP TRAINING
These skaters are performing their dryland jump rotations on the aerobics floor. As with strength training, these skaters are working on their individual jumps/drills, based on their current skill levels. Appropriate floor space, type of floor, and footwear is required for these skaters to train successfully and safely.

weight, without lifting weights. Genetics and increased dietary intake of fat can greatly bulk up the female skater with extra fat, especially at the hip/thigh region. To automatically associate lifting weights with bulking up the skater is a disservice to strength training. If anything, the female skater should use strength training to maintain LBM to increase her skating strength and prevent injury. Lifting weights will help to tone muscles and increase the flexibility and strength of the muscles, bones, soft tissues, and joint areas. A handful of pairs skaters, specifically male pairs skaters, have asked me to design a strength program for the purpose of adding LBM to improve their on-ice performance.

The skater should utilize a well-designed strength program for maintaining LBM and injury prevention, combine endurance (anaerobic) conditioning with bouts of aerobic conditioning for decreasing some body fat, and perform power (plyometric) training when necessary. Finally, and probably the most important recommendation, the skater should monitor dietary intake of fats. The female skater may eventually add bulk (fat) to her body. The key is for that skater to be strong and powerful enough and in peak condition to offset the negative aspects of increased body fat. Finally, adding LBM from resistance strength training depends on exercise choice, volume, intensity, frequency, and rest periods. My main emphasis on strength and power training of skaters is to use more multijoint total-body strength exercises as opposed to isolated movements. Using periodized training and multijoint strength and power exercises minimizes the chances of bulking up the skater. Overall, the strength and conditioning program design is for figure skating, not body-building or football.

What about rest and tapering off? I could write a separate chapter regarding this question. Overall, I do feel that the majority of skaters may not be getting the proper amount of rest throughout the training and competitive year (refer to Chapter 8). Tapering off is necessary for a skater's performance prior to competition, but too often, coaches do not taper off a skater's training. As an off-ice strength coach, I taper off off-ice training at various periods of the training year and for major competitions. Tapering off is an alteration in training frequency, duration, and volume to physically and mentally restore the athlete. Typically, the volume and duration of workouts are reduced; however, intensity is usually maintained, if not increased somewhat. I recommend tapered training at least one and a half to two weeks prior to major competitions (regionals, sectional, nationals, major internationals, worlds, and Olympics).

Specific examples of tapering off on-ice may be a reduction in freestyle sessions or practice time, reduction in total number of jumps performed on the ice, or reduction in total number of program run-throughs per practice sessions. A reduction in training volume (sets times repetitions) and frequency off-ice are suggested. For example, a skater preparing for nationals may perform one to two intense strength workouts with a reduction in volume five to six days before departing for that competition. Finally, skaters should work on flexibility stretching and perform cool-down routines before competitions, as this will be important for performance at the competition. I recommend a reduced volume, moderate- to high-intensity strength workout the day before traveling to a competition,

ELITE SKATER PERFORMING A POWER CLEAN
An elite international-level skater performs a power clean. This strength/power exercise involves a ballistic pulling movement elevating the bar from midthigh to the skater's shoulder level. This technical/explosive exercise involves extension of the ankles, knees, and hips, accelerating the resistance vertically to a held position.

such as regionals, sectionals, nationals, worlds, or Olympics. This is important for strength maintenance throughout that competitive week.

Total rest and active rest should occur throughout the training year, not just during competitive periods. As a coach, you can tell when a skater is saturated both physically and mentally, making a complete rest day necessary. It's important to gain a rest day quickly, versus having the skater continue training without the needed energy levels and enthusiasm. As fatigue sets in, there can be subtle changes in skill technique, which increases the chances of acute injury. Why not let that skater go home to rest and recover, and then come back a day later fully energized? If the skater does reach a state of complete exhaustion and there are symptoms of overtraining, the skater may need weeks to recover. So it's smart to listen to the athlete's body and implement rest days when needed.

Other questions and areas for further investigation or research. The first question that comes to mind is: Are our skaters overtrained or do they reach a point of staleness? Why do so many skaters reach a plateau in their on-ice training for an extended period of time? How much does their physical disposition come into play? Do skaters reach a point in their skating careers where they cannot physically acquire the skills for continued success in the sport? For female athletes, there may be a greater need for supplemental off-ice strength and conditioning training as their bodies go through puberty and mature physically. What about injured skaters that have been off the ice for an extended duration due to serious or even moderate injuries, and return back to the ice too soon and reinjure themselves? Care needs to be taken to make sure the skater is recovered and strong from off-ice strength and conditioning to return to their on-ice training safely.

173

It can be discouraging as a coach to see skaters burn out or get injured one week before a major competition. These problems can be avoided if coaches and skaters take the necessary steps with structured training, periodized training with rest, tapering, balance in training, or consistent off-ice training. We are in a sport that takes kids at an early age, overloads them with instruction and application of finely skilled, complicated techniques, and requires that they repeat those techniques many times to progress. This high volume of repetitions can occur over many years of training. Hopefully, the skater, coach, and parent can take some of the concepts discussed in this book to *facilitate* the total development of the figure-skating athlete. I am not suggesting this as a means to an end, but as a part of the whole.

CHAPTER 1

1. A. Podolsky, et al., "The relationship of strength and jump height in figure skaters," *American Journal of Sports Medicine* 18, no. 4 (1990): 400–405.
2. P. Van Handel, et al., "Observations on skating (laboratory and on-ice testing) implications for training," unpublished material presented at the 1992 Elite Figure Skating Camp, U.S. Olympic Training Center, Colorado Springs, Colo., April 1992.
3. R. M. Brock and C. C. Striowski, "Injuries in elite figure skaters," *Physicians and Sportsmedicine* 14, no. 1 (1986): 111–115.
4. W. C. McMaster, S. Liddle, and J. Walsh, "Conditioning program for competitive figure skating," *American Journal of Sports Medicine* 15, no. 4 (1979): 43–46.
5. V. Niinjmaa, "Figure skating: What do we know about it?" *Physicians and Sportsmedicine* 10, no. 1 (1982): 51–56.

CHAPTER 3

1. C. M. Poe, et al., "Off-ice resistance and plyometric training for singles figure skaters," *Strength and Conditioning*, National Strength and Conditioning Association 16, no. 3 (1994): 68–76.
2. K. L. Lockwood, "Kinetic and kinematic characteristics of impact upon landing single, double, and triple revolution jumps in figure skating," First Congress on the Sports Medicine and Sports Sciences of Skating, San Jose, Calif., January: 19–21, 1996.
3. "Position Statement: Youth Resistance Training," position statement paper and literature review, *Strength and Conditioning*, 62–75, December 1996.

CHAPTER 5

1. C. M. Poe, "Plyometrics: Beneficial for all disciplines of skating, singles, pairs, and ice dance," *The Professional Skater Magazine*, PSA 27, no. 4 (July/August 1996): 19–20.

CHAPTER 8

1. C. M. Poe et al., "Off-ice resistance and plyometric training for singles figure skaters," *Strength and Conditioning*, National Strength and Conditioning Association 16, no. 3 (1994): 68–76.

CHAPTER 9

1. C. M. Poe, "Increasing strength and power without bulking-up," *Skating* 74, no. 2 (February 1997): 70–71.

About the Author

Carl M. Poe was born in Durham, North Carolina, and received his master's degree in exercise science in 1991 from Appalachian State University. He then served as an intern designing strength and conditioning programs for athletes at the United States Olympic Training Center (USOTC). Poe also worked as a sport physiology research assistant for the USOTC, Colorado Springs, Colorado, assisting with physical performance testing and evaluations of elite athletes.

Poe has designed strength and conditioning programs and has trained skaters for eleven years. He has assisted at the United States Figure Skating Association (USFSA) elite sports science camps, Novice Nationals, National Training Camp, Junior Nationals camps, and regional training camps. He has also presented at Professional Education Program (PEP) seminars (Denver) for the Professional Skaters Association (PSA). Poe was the off-ice strength and conditioning coach for national- and international-level skaters at the Colorado Springs World Arena, 1995 to 1997. He is currently director of off-ice strength and conditioning training for skaters throughout the Chicago, Illinois, area and also strength coach of national- and international-level skaters. He serves as a member of the USFSA, USFSA Sports Medicine Committee, PSA, PSA Sports Science Committee, the National Strength and Conditioning Association, and the Wagon Wheel Figure Skating Club.

Poe conducts seminars and off-ice strength and conditioning program development for skating programs throughout the United States. He is also the author of many articles on off-ice and on-ice strength and conditioning training and figure skating. He resides in Buffalo Grove, Illinois, with his wife Robyn Poe (a competitive master-rated figure-skating coach) and their dog Solomon.

Index